"Slaying the Dragon"

By: The President King of All Position: Riley Miller

XXX

Copyright © 2012 Riley Parker Miller

All rights reserved.

ISBN-10:1479347434

ISBN-13: 978-1479347438

This is dedicated to the Holy Spirit And Inside God Of Whose Flesh Of My Flesh Are Inside Which Nothing Could Become Better And More Possible Without God's Son: Jesus Christ

"These Current Approaches And Inside the Dragon's Lair In the Manipulation and the Theories and Its Discoveries Inside Of Anyone Who Is Of These Entire New World Order's Promises And Inside Many Of These Deals Of the New World Order: Comes the Dragon"

By: Riley Parker Miller

Introduction:

The Insanity of slaying the dragon:

In this book I am recruiting for the top people, and these top places, and for these, top positions, in my life that comes from the Dragon, and his lair, that I am not responsible for in any of this, in the lives that are, taken, and then placed on top of the realness, in mankind. The Dragon appears wherever the Dragon goes, and these are seen, and are heard, in these lairs of justice and peace, to the knowledge of the world. We must happen in this way. The looks of the new world order, and strength in the new world order, is better and stronger than the Dragon.

The Very Beginnings In The Progress Of Man

"These National Treasures That Are Inside of the Truest Buried Mind Of the Inventions That Comes From the Inside Of All Of These Lives Of Buried Treasure Inwardly Into the Life of Mine; and Inwards and Towards the Brand Newest, " New Order of the Ages"

I.

One Introduction To the World:

These are the titles anyways and the responsibility comes from the "new world order" and, of these official titles, is from these, dedicated lives to this entire book's philosophical natures, of man inside of God. He is the one and only man we can support, or do well with that, can make sense to the natures of the other mankind. These are the only natures of man which are and can wrap around what can become one's successes, with the new goodness of society.

1. What appears inside the dragon's lair, so what are the questions in the new order of the ages, whenever, it all comes down to monetary values inside experiences:

Toward whoever in relevancy is to the start of a new world order? And, towards whatever are these followers of the new order of the ages and its master plan? Is this toward, the king, or in a dragon's lair, and in his approach that can become what is, in which I have explained, can be easily explained, and the true reality of God's very own good design, better than that of man? The life of mine, can become one of living for it all, if only one true member of the "new world order", would step out, and will take the consequences, for all in these titles, that we have lost, towards a newer Constitution of the United States of America's tradition?

The mirrored reality, of the nation and country, mirrored behind, the things that we have lost, and inside that, in which we have found, and, inside of all; that we all have been discovering, comes an brand new and, hopefully known, reality, inside of, the very great God's issues inside man? This in, is about and of, these plans, offered to only one in his, very own, master, in the world, of the new order of the ages? Hopefully all of this sense, is coming from, one source, that is inside the United States government's clients?

1. What does it take to, create the world around you, after you defeat the dragon, and these nature and able-bodied people, who have, in whatever are the answers, to the new world order's, greatest financial answers, that are all gone:

There are worries, for whatever is inside, of all of these insides, in these ostensive and the manual on the radars, of policemen's cars, that do not have, a cause other than, arresting all of us, and them as well in, the manner of society in which brought them up. This is in, that other than whatever, resource can, can become defined as "saintly". This is from the United States' government. The real Uncle Sam's hideout needs a place to learn. The world is about new and old government, and, inside of how we can get judged, by others. We all need ourselves, and lives sorted out, to become greater, to make it a cleaner and better, American position. I can and will dig out any, of the worms as soon as, the world would close down. What, these are and is about becomes in the lights, of the academics, and the quality, and, the learning, that, has defined the "light", from where this stands, and, towards in the afterlife there is an afterlife for, ourselves; in the light of Godliness, in man. This is the light of imperfection. These are, in the life of God. This is about and of my old high school, called the "Highland Park High School" within God and the students therein, that can learn and teach, better than the average status quo, or very, very high above, this level's quotient in students, that is inside the better grades, than more people, on the high of the mountains, of academics. These are the nooks and crannies that the world government will come from, inside it all. This is about and of the revelations.

2. Whatever are in the good, and the evil, whereof there are the qualities, and quantities of the new order of the ages, that can come alive, or dead in these, answers inside these lives of mine where chance and opportunity go together:

These master plans, of the entire new order of the ages, have been moot or blank for the past few years that I have, planned this out, of the common man's good. These are in the good ideas of man. Accordingly, neither actors nor pretenders may ever buy into the "good news", of the newly formed, the new order of the ages in its master. This is not a hide-and-go seek, or a "peek-a-boo", but is a newly sprung individualism, and inside these fond aware masterpieces, of my every desire and perfections, that are simple in the years of our lives, that are inside and of my life to live, and inside of my one and only lives towards living, comes the directions that we were not seeing straight in the first way. These are in, and of, these angles of perfection, and, these masters of design, that are spinning, each and every ways, and the angles, and of the designed outcome, and in, my every man's mankind's piece of the guilty and gutted, within the shark, comes the "real bait". The "baits", are that which, are of the government. Thereof there lies on every immediacy, a thought, and into every thought, an active individual, and to every active person, a newer country, and, a newer breathtaking, and very aware day of our lives. This is about and is in these businesses that are, of mine.

The goals of mankind: These inner realities, and the spheres of influence, are in the new world order, are located for the good, in man.

II. The Second, And the Third Introduction Towards In All; Of These Top Book's Influences In Saving, the Graces Of God:

To each of all, of us who must have something to follow or to own, in life, comes the progress of God, that has saluted us all. Towards getting there, we must scale out of the dragon's lair. This is a simple and complex, story. This is about mine. I am President King of all; Riley Miller: for overcoming the dragon's lair. This used to be like me, but now I am a Christian-follower, of Christ the Lord.

I have and am a Christian follower, because of the ways that the one and only, Christ the Lord, has saved me, from the hellish existences, in mankind. This is where I would have gone wrong, if it were not, for Jesus Christ. This is, anyways, and always for the blood of the Lamb. This is how and in where He saved me!

To get out of the 'dragon lair', I would need to have George W. Bush Jr. for, the buying, of the real and, whole plans, of mine, into the new world order, of a certain five gentlemen. I have listed five to seven men, on the new world order, in the sheets of mine. They also, must scale greatness, which is in their minds. This is to get the dragon outside, on the outsides, of the sides of the current temple.

I am the personable person, and a real person, in the deal, of the plan to purchase, towards the plans, to the purchases, of the new world order, with notes of greatness. These are, the words, and notes, that the music must play to defeat the dragon. These are the notes of harmony, and, gracefulness, in, where time and space, and I can live.

These are in Riley Parker Miller, and his attainable conquests, to own the world, inside of world ownership, and into owning the whole world, with harmony. These are, not from the dragon, but are from Jesus Christ. These are not from the dichotomy, of good and evil, but from, the good life. These are from the followers of mine in every city. This is, what every Christian, should have accomplished, because of God, in these lives, of who can take the original shoes, and put them on the soles, of, the original disciples. Whichever lives are and is in and of, the new order of the ages. This is inside, me.

These outcome able plans, on, the new world order, are based on Riley Miller's life's goals, in the challenges, or in the lives of mine, to control the real world deal, of the supernatural, and the natural resources, in the world, and, to always buy, and control all of the money, forever, it seems. I am not a "Dr. Evil", but I am, Riley Miller. I will try to control and own, the entire world. If this is possible, then it is possible through George W. Bush.

If you like these company concepts, that, I can show you, then, forever and, forever five thousand, or more, company concepts, inside, these businesses and these companies, that, I can sell to the entire government, in the world. This is the beginning, of the new world order.

We can, and will, sell and grow and appear, within, and without this "new order of the ages", to overnight, and towards, these businesses, and, all of these, companies, of the new world order, that there are lives, and, there are deaths in, forever, of all. There are from the likelihood, of the order, in businesses, and, inside the lifetimes, of literatures; that you will have at the beginning of lifetimes', the very own, apparatus and, its own functioning, that can, control the world, and these entire natural resources of the world.

III. The real book's introduction in the cause and explanation, on the values in mankind's mottos and lives in which we all, can touch and can explain to each other, what it is to be a Christian; in Jesus Christ:

<u>These are and is the living properties of one man, and another man, and also another woman, that can, keep the clean, and sober living of life; the new world order.</u>

<u>I can belong to these wins. The win is over evil. These wins and losses are over evil. There are always evil ones.</u>

Welcome to the New World Order-

These Are the Beginnings and Belongings, to the Treasures, in the Book On Life; On The Questions and Answers, of the Futures of Inventing and, Business Endeavors Inside the Realm of Inventing: These Accolades That All Are Mine, And That Are For Sale:

A new world order has emerged, to cover and control the entire world, and planet. I, have seen over thousands and thousands, of articles on the emergence, of a new world order, on all over, the Internet, within thousands of people's opinions, and, thoughts about an, official, new world order. I, plan on starting this new world order.

One, quotation is from, George H. W. Bush; pertaining to the "new world order", out of every President who has talked about it when he said:

"Today that new world is struggling to be born, a world quite different from the one we have known. A world where the rule of law supplants the rule of the jungle. A world in which nations recognize the shared responsibility for freedom and justice."

This supplements, the "Riddles of the Sphinx", which is inside how we will control the natural resources, and, in however to control the world, also. The endeavors, to control the natural resources, he mentioned in his speech.

The quote is about the new world order.

A "Riddle of the Sphinx", and in this life, and into these times; there are and is many questions and answers. To have this comes to mind; I solved the riddle of the sphinx when I was driving once. It was, "to always know what you are doing", "no matter what the circumstances are". Now, I feel more enlightenment, and then much better off, knowing what this is, about God. It is that God is the only person who knows what He is doing, in the midst of all this madness. This is to know what you are doing inside yourself, no matter what the time and place. The riddle of the sphinx of the new world order's outlooks is, to always survive. It is even in times of, either new war, or, new peace, inside the world.

I am Riley Parker Miller. The basic introduction of this is for the new world order. I have a boat a car and a house. Actually, I have none of these possessions, as much as others, because none, of them, are in and of my concern, just yet. This is, about the life of mine, and in how I have created the new world order. I have many different company offers, and, properties, within the entire new world order world government, for sale.

I have many business offers that are, all for the one world government, of the new "new world order" of, the very official "one world government". This is about the responses and issues, which are made and are in the real "world government", of mine. This is about and in the motion of the changing of the whole entire world's landscape, with businesses, buildings, new phenomenal planning, a new government outline, and an entire new world order, of my constructions. But, for now this is all on written papers, with deals yet to come true to me and for you. I also, have plans for every political party, across the globe.

I am discussing about the <u>University of Oxford</u>, and the secret societies therein which I can create, at the bottom of this page, through my writings, in the realities, that are, in these zillion dollar inheritances, that are of, mine. This book is mostly, a sort of a, mostly famous book ever written, within these writings, and inside these businesses, that are in what take a look, and, inside these good creations that make the world have, all, that is inside another good book, that are and is about God.

I have an invention list at the bottom, of the book, and about the new world order, and, the secret societies, that I can explain to you, only listed here, in the book's total messages inside life, and in these, items are the livingness, in the life, that seems to be in my hands. These are hard working hands.

Let me explain to you, let there be no confusion or hypocrisy, but I am the best writer inside of the world new world order, and my sixty six books, and over, seventy publications on the new world order.

I will explain here, these inventions, and, these secret societies, of the new world order, and all about the new order of the world, no matter, how or, what you call it, in these lives of mine. Inside the contexts, and, inside the book, I mention and talk about the zillions of dollars, and a one world government, of these orders, of the new order of the ages, that I am not talking about being, unprepared or unready for, but I, am talking about, peace and love, for the whole world. This comes from my inventive mind, and the deeds of inventions, and the necessities in life, which balance and harmonize that of the life of businesses, in the insides, in the life, of all of mine.

These real contexts, of this book are rather unusual, because it is about the new world order. This is not a silly and funny topic, but a frame of mind. These are about Oxford University, and how I want a free-ride scholarship from George W. Bush Jr. to start this here, and in the world, and all over the whole world. This is not the death of the world, or, from and in, an unusual way, of looking inside life, of looking into the bigger picture of the new world order, from the University of Oxford, to the new world order, and into, the "Associated Individual's Clubs" of the new world order. This is about the "University of Oxford's" outlines, and, inside of, the made contexts, and into these lives of mine, where the streets have no name, to, where in the oddities of the world, the streets do have the hidden code. This is behind, the improvements of the world, and, but that in and about the University of Oxford's knowledge, and the abilities, of there within.

This is not an obsession or a fascination, but whatever I have done with this, in living is in whatever, I can do, and I want to own the world, through the mediums, of these secret societies, the endeavors, and inventions, and, lastly businesses, inside the life of mine. These are not about the freemasons or the skull and crossbones yet. I plan on, starting clubs, in which are simple and the complex, and am similar to these secret societies inside these manners and these fashions, inside the reality, and fiction world.

The book is for my storybook fans. These are not the "most simple", God fans, which have ever been around. Nope. They are not talking about just anything but smarter things and even the wisest and not the most simplest man inside of the history of the world could not even think of math without these alliances there could not be stronger members that participated in the world moreover in the insanity of the real one who did not write in this book. I think that Riley Miller's mind was not a simpleton product but a stronger man and in a blanket and a towel and the perfectionist and a know-it-all. This is not from the "New World Order" or the "New Order of the Ages". All this was came from anything but the wishing well I wished upon when I was younger, as a kid.

The world has a good and an unusual game and a record and a way of playing that game to its own music and that is especially chosen in the terms of one and another one book and another book. One person can see into the other person and know exactly what they are talking about when the music plays. The terms that are in the world of knowledge are inside and of the one thing and not the other thing unless one's person understands what the other person is talking about in the sense of reality and in the sense of the common man. The one in this hand is inventing and another man on this other hand is secret society.

One bad man once said that the road that is not traveled on is not the good road no matter what you think and say to another person's lie. The one in the one hand is not the right person if you do not think that he is the right person. And on another hand the one who does not think he is right might not be able to help it. The one road that is less traveled on does not mean that it is necessarily the wrong road. The one road that leads you to another road does not really mean that it is the right road and usually one person does not know about the other person unless it is wrong for him. These are the right instructions for one person to not follow another person unless they are not ever right.

In the long run one road does not lead you to another right road unless there are two equal people. This is about the two kinds of people who are not right and are not wrong but in the end the two roads lead you to one another no matter what the other person said. The point is that in inventing there are two roads you cannot take: the secret society and the best way with inventing.

These are the two roads that we are not traveling on yet. The first road is the one that is less traveled on and the second road is the road, which the two of us have never seen. The one road is too small to travel on and the second road is the one that we cannot even see. The first one that is ready to use traveling on is the first road that is ready for us to use. But then the next road to travel on is the next road that we are ready to use.

What if both roads are under construction? Would this make sense to one member of the road if it were a "secret society"? No the first member of the road is an inventor. That means that the second person in the second road does not have any place to go.

God's own, very predestined natures, of the world, are in the Divine Immaculate Conception Plan's incredible designs, and supreme looks. The one person and the other person have not made and cannot use in any sense unless the road was already designed for you.

--The Book--

These Endings, Of The Beginnings Of The New World Order Of The "Associated Individuals Clubs" From The Founder From A Project And An Outline From An Insane Man's Outcomes Becomes The Wonder Of The World In Fictional Outlooks And The Insanity Of Mine. This Book Is About To Create This. This Is Altogether To Turn The World Around. I am not kidding I want to start all of the secret societies of the world.

These are from the insides and from these simplistic invention's forms inside of the book's messages and thoughts that are to clear one's mind and to not let him think of the insanity. This is about and of the messages of the factual existences that can exist and do not exist and should exist. A new thesis of these simplistic formations of the basic thoughts and of mankind possesses and can have knowledge in existential forms. There are the shown existences and are in the living proofs that man can have these certain characteristics from the directions in his life that should change into the dreams and fictions of man and his fellow primate or his fellow animals.

THESE ARE IN THE SECRET SOCIETY'S HANDBOOKS AND ON THESE REALITY'S ENGINEERED TOPICS OF INVENTING AND IN HOW IN LIFE AND IN HOW I CAN MAKE A SINGLE DOLLAR.

I HAVE BECOME WITH A RECORD BREAKING CLUBS STARTERS AND A REAL PERSONAL INVENTOR THROUGHOUT MANKIND AND HIS VOYAGE TO THE HIGH SEAS. THESE ARE THE SIMPLISTIC THINGS THAT ARE INSIDE OF THE CLUB'S RESOUNDING STARTERS THAT CAN CREATE ANEW OR THAT CAN BECOME INSIDE DIFFERENT WAYS THAT CAN MAKE WAVES AND SHOULD BE RESOUNDINGLY GOOD FOREVER INSIDE OF THESE DIFFERENT SHOES.

THE SECRET SOCIETY AT THE LIFE OF WHATEVER I CAN DO WITH INTELLIGENCE AND INTO THE LIFETIMES AND THE DEATHS OF THE SECRET SOCIETY AND ITS CALLING INSIDE OF THE GENTLE AND HUMANE WORLD. THIS COMES FROM A SHARP MIND AND A KEENER INTELLECT.

THESE ARE THE FIRST MANUAL EVER TO GET TO KNOW INTO THESE DAYS AND INTO THESE LIVING FOREVER LIVES AND INTO ALL OF THE INTELLECTUALLY KNOWING AND VERY SUBSTANTIALLY KNOWN DEATHS THAT ARE INSIDE OF THESE DAYS INTO THE NEW WORLD ORDER'S VERY FIRST BEGINNING FOREVER. THIS BEGAN FROM THE FIRST MOMENT AND THEN FROM WHAT BECAME A REVOLUTION CAME ONE MAN. HE WAS THE MAN WHO STARTED THE REVOLUTION: ME. I AM THIS PERSON.

All of this madness inside life goes towards these games in life and inside and towards the callings that are inside and in all of the real "new world order" and in and, going forwards into the books and magazines there are past Presidents and Kings. Within the life of mine and within the library's book volumes there are all of the funny things and that inside the typically known shoe store there is always an all-star employee or the worker for the new world order's personality with a good membership. This is in my perfect world and inside of the good life and is in what I hope in life that I can barely and only imagine. This is of the freedoms and the peaces of all peoples in the worlds. I have the New Order of the Age's, first books. The books are inside the inventions, and the businesses, in the books. These are the fictions, and realities, in the world.

These are the unseen, images and failures, in successes and the obscene failures that are the college or a university might bring. In all of it that it brings I hope that forever in all of the "selective membership" of the games and constant directions of these lives there are forever people's lives inside of the "new world order" inside games and events that are not in whatever can all count for college, and for everyday life and that the book seller's world, revolves, and rotates, and turns rightfully, into all, of these endeavors. I am not saying that I am a very true nonbeliever or a confused person but I have seen and heard the real believing from a fundamentalist Christianity wise, point of view. I am not and am saying that I am a real and very good, and the successful man, in this life, and in these lives of mine. I have not, the quality and quantity for, the goodness into and inside, the "new world order", but in, the only God, am in the real Jesus Christ.

Whatever in life where there are can become the hope for the reality of the lost people in the world's visions and into the very versions inside and of the reality in the "new order of the ages" and its victories? These are in the inventing and the finding, inside, oneself and in life and in a newer life become more successfully, prone in, these ways in the Biblical manner: to succeed.

And in the successes and the failures and of the lives unto the real successes and in wealthy occupations in all their wealth and, inside and, for their needs and in the needs of others in former lives that are all around the world's intellectuals, known towards, the world of where these certain and in all of these distinguished people, who can see and can know that they live.

This is the no-brainer within life. There is a calling and a summoning for the new world order. All of these top people have gone through initiations and have gone through forever throughout my, whimsical and late starting secret societies that have also done well and have all made it in life's generalized calling. This is of the nutritionist and a player, in, mind control, of these others. This is not about, the cults.

In memory of and to the best former Presidents in the past President's lives, a history has been, lost and gone, and not discovered. This is of that is whatever; we have the fond and the greatest memory of our life that is for the best Presidents in the history of the world's greatest.

I have been inspired to write all of this towards your lives. This is in order to understand you better and towards this to even knowing your world a much and small little better. And in this life and inside your world may there be all in this action togetherness very well known promises. This is that we all can forever keep all of the promises, in the world the same. This is about the kingdom of Heaven and, in how we, will inherit, it all.

This is, inside the world. There, are the past kingdoms of the world, and its inheritance, that is only Jesus Christ.

In the traditions in life and inside the knowledge of the world there lies one man. This is from and in first history in the world to a last history. To use a better word "tradition" or "excellence". These are from the victories of the outcomes and the superior outlooks that are in and of the new 'new world order'. I still have to claim the victory that becomes in Christ that we all have won and I have won so many years ago.

Within and without using too much knowledge and from this good intelligence we all have tried to write and to produce a "new world order" manual or "outline". This is in the outcomes inside of goodness, inside, methodology of a sheet's rulebook that is in mine and is in man. This is all mines and is toward another new real family tradition in the spirit of my only fathers. These are the founding fathers of the United States of America.

The greater life and in its challenges to beginning to write to yourself the <u>New Order of the Ages'</u> Scriptures within these pages into its sheets and in the world and from its real writing can come secrets. These are for you; "President Lincoln" and the sheets that I can write to you and inside of those that are from me in mine life. I can and in very much wellness it should do these ventures in the placements of the "New Order of the Ages" in the consent and in inner productions within, these mankind's real values inside God.

These famous titles and positions of the better-known issues can come from taxicabs and cigarettes. Just make sure we are not very annoying. This is inside the primal instinct.

I have done the immediate creating and the foremost in and of whatever it is that I have universally known and have done in being in which have been consumed inside making and producing these world agendas inside of mankind's creations. From this these are and obsessively in the new world order I had been creating the first and foremost all brand new creation in the United States of America's pleasant futures and in the past history baseballs.

Whatever in one life's one means in the reality of the "one world government" and from and inside these great and very strict laws and, outcomes, statutes in the America's outcome becomes God and one God in one way. He is from these briefer statutes of man and the plans on me in this real financial endeavor of God. These are of and in these accounts of the accolades of God.

The United States of America has a big time deal with all of this inspiration in whatever has inspired so and very much of me towards writing the new world order has been kings. This has been the write of this inside a new format and fashion which many people's brains for the traps of the politicians that have done well with our new country's outlooks.

These are inside these United States of America's world Constitutional governments, that are based, and largely started, inside of the United States of America's zillion dollars and futuristic outlooks, and in began man, and inside of these victories, of God's triumphs; come another man. These are and in from the United States. This is a new and stronger country.

NEW WORLD ORDER'S VERY REAL PROGRESSES IN THE SACRED AND WORTHWHILE OPPORTUNITY AND FOREVER THE BRIGHT FUTURE IN THE INVENTIONS AND THESE VERY PROMISED OUTCOMES AND INSIDE AND FOR THESE AMERICAN TRADITIONS COME OF THE BLANDLY NEW COMPROMISING SITUATIONS INSIDE OF THE COMPROMISES IN THE FUTURE OF THE REAL MAN'S OUTCOMES. : FOREVER IN THE NEW WORLD ORDER'S PROMISE OF THE AGES OF MAN THESE CLEAR RESOLUTION IN THE NEW WORLD ORDER OF MAN--

FOREVER THESE ARE THESE REAL HUNDREDS OF TRILLIONS OF THESE REAL DOLLARS COME FROM THE UNITED STATES OF AMERICA'S REAL BRIGHT FUTURE. THAT NEW AMERICAN FLAGS COMES THE TRADITIONS FROM THE ZILLIONS. HAVE I MADE IT INSIDE OF THAT WHICH IS A NEW COUNTRY'S BEGINNINGS AND THESE TRUE ENDINGS; INSIDE THE PROGRESS OF MAN? INSIDE OF THE KNOWLEDGE OF THE DECLARATIONS OF THE NEW BEGINNINGS IN MAN COME OF THE AGE OF MANKIND AND MAN'S FORWARD PROGRESS; THESE ARE INSIDE OF THE NEW WORLD ORDER'S SECOND COMING TO EARTH. OF WHAT WE CAN BE DOING FOREVER FOR SUCH A COUNTRY THAT WE A HAVE LOVED; FORWARD PROGRESS IN THE MOTION OF THE NEW WORLD ORDER?

THE NEW WORLD ORDER HAS ALREADY MADE IT TO THE ENTIRE WORLD, OF THE INTERNET AND MAN. I WOULD LIKE TO SELL IT TO THE UNITED STATES OF AMERICA.

These "One World Government" promises and victories in the United States of America, and it's real future could have whatever is in us all of us and ever since we began, in it all and could own this new order of the ages', newness promises and dictations for this country's future soul's everlasting, power.

Oneself, inside life, and, into the insides of whatever, inside of one's, immediate and very own country with all of the Constitutions and all of these, written laws and all of these zillions of whatever in the new order of the ages' for the calling from what it is on the almighty dollar's value within the real dollars.

These are inside of the framework the new Constitution, and the new 'one world government', that has settings of us all, in the dollar bill's treasured content, in the symbol, of "Novus Ordo Seclurum"? Does this country make any sense at all to any one of us and how this is done? These lives in the United States that are concluded and then made to do this justified of mine are of and about these living structures of peace and justice that God can see how and how we have to have these structures and buildings built?

I am the "Riley Miller" and in this life a normal Christian protestant citizen of the United States of America can be owned and can, variously, keep owning the various parts of the world.

This is about the traffic and in the bigger and the better realities of the car. These are in and of the myths of King David. Was he only a man? Did he actually own the world? Only in one man who has got as rich as I want to be is "King Solomon". This is either himself or "King David".

King David must have had a lot of friends. They all probably showed up at his birthday parties. There are the numbers and the peoples in the king's temple and in that there were guards and there were servants and there were magicians and there was the king himself of all the lands that the eyes could see. This was through and to the ways that were through the manifestations and purely sinful natures in the man's heart. This was before that he learned in how to get zillions? We must double check God and this person's human heart before we talk about the zillions. These are made for fun and entertainment. This is on with the show.

These are into money lives and into the monetary lives can bring the gap much closer towards the gaps in the monetary of mine because I am very poor. The money systems and the money gaps have become a lot smaller for most people. This was in the last on three years. I think inside life we need more of a man to balance out the budget.

The reality and the titles of the "king of all" needs to always restructure his life in order to get his throne back. The "President King" should be a new position in the government. This is from and of all power's power. The absolute power of this is outrageous. This is from one central government. This is from the one central government of the "real one". This is from me "Riley Miller". I must very well start and successfully run a one-world government. This is by the people and for the people. This is by the money and for the power. This is an entire and complete government unity built over night. This is about and in the government of the peoples that are of these peoples that are for these peoples of the night. We, have what are all for each other, in the new world order, and the new order of the ages, the context of Jesus Christ, and the calling of God. One centralized unifying person leads the charge. This is into the hell the heaven and, then back. This is of the one centralized government and the one centralized bank that we must own and control and operate together. This will have no fussing around. This will be the unified central government. There will be no need for lack of money or lack of power. The unity will start and will continue forever.

In the times of need and in the lives of the government; comes Riley Miller. These are his statues and his army of the darkness of mankind. There is the King David and the picturesque settings of the pictures that are in the insides in his life in the all of the Holy Ghost's living structures and in the Holy Bible's reality of the pictures of the reality of the harsh ways of the very own mankind. In his temples and of the castle wall's picturesque pictures and inside of God and of these greater pictures there are always inside and of Jesus Christ and in the life and mine and into these real phrases and for these pictures comes the real praises for the God that becomes God.

He is in the ending the end of King David. He is in the self of you. And in the government and in all of these tongues sings "nobody's perfect" and into the world and towards the lights of the dawn of the Christianity of the man's lives means that no one is perfect.

And in that which becomes of all of his light is into the real darkness of the government and in the "real person's government" and this is into a more greater adventure and in all in this and in another version is a greater step towards the questions for man's real eternal questions and the answers therein and of the lights and of the man's victories and triumphs and what is in God comes man's greatest adventures.

This is in and from the goodness of the Godliness of the Harvest the real God of the saving of man's life, and newly claimed lives. There are the lights and in and what are from these are inside in whatever are in the newly created governments inside of this newly created body and the light from the creations of for whatever becomes in whatever is inside the offered truths and the fallen man.

Ask of what you are made of and you are always with the insides of these deaths and of the codes and in liberty and justice and in whatever are in and towards into the holistic values that are from the inventions of mine. There all in this comes love. This is about the brotherhood servitude and the marches of the dawn of, this march of dimes. This is from the real King David and his rise to power. This is about how he had slain Goliath.

One Person's View of the World Government's Properties

This is the real enemy of the government and the real enemy of man. He is in the giant. The government is of the giant, who has always slain Goliath. Yet nobody does do the slain of it. This is about the Johnson and Murphy shoes. I have only worn these in Chicago. I am scared to death to start the world government. The world has better shoes on than me so why wait inside and why don't I start the "one world government". These are the best plants in the garden that can grow. These are in and of the true King David. He has argued himself silly in the Bible to be a king and almost the king of all kings.

This is in what is in store for the position in me. David the King was the most trusted and most reliable king to ever walk the earth. In his shoes were some previous kings and then in his footsteps was Jesus Christ. He rose to the occasions and killed Goliath once. This was about the proving of the life and the "one world democracy" of the "one world government" will be a "no big surprise" unto the world's stage.

There will be no one world war and there will be no "one world democracy" and there will be no "one world government" without the surplus of the entire world's money in this gradual increase of power. The "one world's government" has the entire world working for it. These are of the parables that Jesus Christ once taught. It was in however to be the most powerful man, in the world.

The Christianity of the soldier of Goliath was as shaky as the tender root of the thread of the upheld root that had no water and that had no soil. The Goliath giant has been taken down that is forever!!

The government has started. This is what is being built from the building from the ground up. This is from the first level to the very tops of the building. These are in the groups and in the dynamics of the man who wants to build and to create the government all for him.

He dies on the rocky road. This man does not endure forever and forever he is cursed because he is the man to build the tower taller than God. This is about the man who tries to mess with us in this real situation of the starting of the world government or so that it seems when this is not in and altogether true that is about truthfulness and the lies from therein; that can bring us to the grave. The man who built the world government has to apologize.

From parts of David and Goliath and in the Holy Bible's messages that are for this and these are inside of one Christ and in me alone is Him the real one and chosen person to take down the roots of the seed of David and to plant a new seed and to gain a newer throne. This is of what is kind and of love and is kind of eventful and for these everlasting values of the God in and of the world's greatest inside of all that is inside the most honest and the most braver and the truest man in the Godliness in the factor of God.

I am in the government and only for the gentleman's government's requests and in what is inside the requests of these one world government's eternal questions are inside the Eternal Blog of the eternal answers that become in whomever is inside the Holy Scriptures of all of the Scripture Bibles and is not merely of the name of Jesus Christ but in the name of the one and truest power. The one world government will supposedly start very small and appear very big. The "one world government" was part of the world's conquests to start smallest and gain and get into the biggest.

The: "one world government" is also aware in the namely: Riley Miller. I am in the eternal questions in the manly conquests in the realms of the real and very own big name of God. He is in Texas and He becomes inside of the man's government.

The eternal questions and pictures are from the domino's effect and from its entire entirety in all of these questions come the answers to Jesus Christ. He is inside this book's endings.

Who is in the past and the near future's "new world government" that has been made to disconnect from all of the one world's societies and the honors of the world that are if not represented by the one world government will leave. This is inside and in it's all and in it's all is always God going into and into the real heart of the one and the unity in God. This is in the God and this is about and of one's most sovereign God that is in the roots that are inward in the planted soil of and in how we may grow together in and to "Kings" and the position of "President King". We must grow bigger and more effectively within government.

The real world government is not ready for this One World Government" procedures and the matters. People are not ready for the one person who decides in this and in who builds the entire structure of something like the likes of: the remnants of "Babylon". We are challenged and are about the one world government and in how the real God lives in this life and in whatever is in the basic introductions to the world's governments are into the world's sins and into these graves becomes deaths: there leads to the most broken of all of the sins in the world.

This is in the Holy Bibles and are in this location and place that is in the God of the entire government who becomes wherever is in the lives of which are not from whomever behaves more very well. This is inside the sins, of the great "Babylon".

These are in and of the golden tribute treasures into whatever is inside the quests of these Holy Bibles and inside whatever is towards the questions and the questions therein of and in the Holy Bibles that goes into whatever is inside and in these everyday days of the Christian. Asking and having the questions, which are made into, be the bitter end to the traveler and inside the tastes of the God. This is about and of the Holy Scriptures. This is of and in the Godly designs in Christianity's most valuable treasures: the cross of Jesus Christ.

This is of the Holy Bible in God. This is from and is for the made pictures and the ready requests of the Holy Bible. This is from and of the "Holy Scriptures" of the Holy Bible of the Holy Word.

The real Holy Bible of God and in the life of God and in the insides of the qualities of the questions and in the inner realities of the requests of the realities of the many of these inventions to the man of these certain ideals inside mankind's legends that are to not be opened in the truth of the man inside the expressions of God. These are from and in whatever are in whatever and are not and from the preexisting qualities inside of the eternity of this Internet Blog in the hopes of the higher forms of a God of all. This comes from these formations and from the actions and in the sentences of these structures of God comes man that is located in Christ. This is in the God of all in Christ and inside the man of God.

I did not very actually and very realistically did what I proposed to these accented ideals that are in the main stream of water and I did not ever want to be in what I was in the needed for and in this structure and in the proposed topics and of the reality of the code languages of the reality are not only in the topics of the world war and the sacred God but in the real world of life of us all that there are from God's pride and joy of whatever is in these cold and hot and warm   qualities that could not ever be in an eternity of the big enough and possibility big enough to satisfy the every quintessentially needed meal inside the needed qualities of the qualities in the God of all; from where is in the world and inside the best inventions of the world.

There are quality times and the mathematics and sciences and arts and of one zillion dollars which are in tribute are within the money in God's wrath and in anger and in bitter and in distaste. There are some within the games that within God; there could become and should become in the challenges of the life of God and in whatever are in this can be a rid of this proposal's outcomes in the realities of the numbers of the hundreds of quantities of the man within the one true mans very real games in the soul satisfying matters of it all in life's shell. The life's real matters and the distaste into the material compositions of the life and inside of mine and these goals in all of the triumphs and in these lives are within the God that are within the soul are within the satisfying matter of it all.

This is inside whatever should become to get the rid of this completely matter of our holistically related values and in our lives; within and of our truly very own qualities on the number and of the name of man from therein and deep within the values and the treasures of the chest of lives come gold bars that is inside the living sense in that all of God and in all of the real one Jesus Christ there is a reality of the gold of the man in his very coughing and lungs disease.

These are in this situational quality that are and is inwardly inside the values and costs of the costs associated purchases of today inside the values of the humanitarianisms in the qualities thus are of within the real mankind's qualities that are of these needed events in the God of all. This is inside of what comes inside the quality and in the insides of the race are of the locations of the other sided man's locations of the day in mine that is totally ready for anything in the enlightening qualities of the man of God.

In the values that are in this country in what are of the "United States of America" there are no reasons for the wars and in these capitalistic views of the areas of the ways of the some motivated peoples that are coming from the wars. And in this new reasons for the faith in God forward to getting into the point that there are in whatever we all have in more reserves of the dollars than in the selected services and in that motivated energy inside and of this numbers qualities in the selected training of the "governmental soldier reserves" in the life of mine that these are the soldiers of fortune. This is of the governmental life.

I just proposed inside of one of the most ever helpful zillions of the worldly ideas and in what is in the most, in the sense, of the capitalism, in the worldly money in value there are no such thing as the reserves and no such things for five zillions of entirety of the dollars of America. There are into these fives to twenty fives or so on some from one start of one dollar bill onto or some off other number of the staffs.

Within our life and of our zillions of the dollars in the dollars of the American traditions I have seen and about I heard of the best into these measures of the amounts and on the insides of the dollars and cents for the Department of State and inside of these realities and these forwarded zones can these becomes and are in the treasure's chests of money and of knowledge and ability in the costs of the America's dollar.

These are in the world's finest qualities of life that are inside the ideals or of the large costly "New Order of the Ages" and in this fresh wind more nature. Inside and in and of the order of the sphinx and in this treasure are the ways within to the abused and humbled real and sacred lists of the real and bigger inside time of the "humankind efforts" that we are handling and have that in what is in life whatever reaches out to the distances towards the issues of the fresh start in mankind. This is for the fresh mints whereof in zillions are in the limits of the cash money's issuance of the proper and immediate remote amounts to the measures of the man in the sense of the very selective "five or more zillions of dollars" that are in real cash. I have been in need and I am in need of some financial cash assistance that is of in God.

I have the elite proposals to make in order to own the Federal Reserve Bank of God the United States of America's treatise. This is in the win in these issues and these values in the tides of everyday' and the happenings that are already in God from these happenings and in whatever are inside there in whatever is from whereof within what are the forms of the revenues and the sources of the inspirations of all that is of and is in this and in these inspirations and these methods inside of God and in these inner lives in whatever is in it all that are inside these fractions inside the mathematics of man in this issue of the aluminum titanium needle that gets the fresh and red blood. Inside of wherein there is some small-minded mathematics comes the light out of whatever there comes what is in the reality of the choices of these very real outcomes and in and always; of the reality becomes one of the reality's challenges of one of the necessities and of one man in man that is in these real items offered the change in life from lives. This is from and in if I can and we can become a zillionaire.

And all which is of it all is offered to this determinism and is of and is inside these victims of circumstance in the people in who they are the real victims of this all; which is forever for God. These are in and of the changes of the reality of the "chosen life" inside and of the deaths and inside and of the "all" that there does become with whatever is a chance of the one's choice inside of "one life". This is about the one life that does not have the one real chance to have all of the riches in America. We are in must one really think and know inside these chess pieces that are in the forever's of it essentially and quintessentially all that we have inside treasures have the riches and the necessary means into having it all.

Then and in all of the Presidential appeal in which I am asking for a zillion dollars of cash with are in the United States of America's tradition and are for and in the treasured and the real life of it all of the zillions of the American tradition! This is of and inside of the dollars and the cents of the American's real tradition and in not imagined solely traditions of the good of all that is inside the sole endeavors of our world. There are for all of the many zillions in cash within the zones and this of its secret codes and the secretive languages of the real numbers in the codes in man's government's traditions in all of these entireties and of this in all in what is of its expense in whatever can become one of whatever becomes in those issues of that negative expense and in which are for the money's place and in the life of mine.

This is in soldiers and in the mercenaries that are for living are for the world's life values and in the history of the government in the all-encompassed doubtfulness and mercy of this money in the statutes are in that which are in and from and are for the message and dictation of modern man in the fictions inside life. The insides and the outsides of the interrelated monies in the monetary gain of red, white, and blue comes monetary values.

This is about and the products that I have been writing for and then saving for writing to come save us to do us a bigger success than anyone ever in the remote histories of the world. This is in what is saying in the investing of the least of the monies and in the insides of these treasures of it that comes and goes in factions. For whatever is not about and in the selling of the yards for it are for the shapes of the zillions of dollars in the cash of the United States of America can come controlled by life.

This is the life in what can detail the "yellow brick road's image and façade to the greatest issues of the modern day marvel of modern man in history's revealing portrait that we are also of natural "togetherness". This life inside can detail the cooks and the chefs of the everyday party of the tongues and forks and knives. There is the daily select utensil for the everyday mix of the modern day zillionaires.

These are the details of these lives and into these lives there is no stranger and there are no more strangers that can dictate and control our lives. This is from and in the "Constitution of the United States of America" and its traditions from "sea to shining sea". These are about the Constitutions of the old world and the new world order and of the Bill of Rights types of laws that are supposed to be already there but we are decreasing from this rule of law in the new order of the ages. This is in schools and of schools there are but what is in the manner and matter of my opinions and propositions that I do not do the Bill of Rights and in the proposed outcome of the outcomes in the US Constitution there are the rule of the civil laws. This is of a new set of laws that are to be construction oriented in built and without forms these traditions of these code languages of some very elite and secretive kinds of groups of people can be living and alive in mankind. That sentence comes from and into the formats and inside the thinking and in about the zillions that are supposed to become mine. All of these issues are in my right pocket and in secret hidden codes that by now we can become healed of the initiations of the rights of the Americas. These come forward in the satisfactions that are in and of the sense that in and of the zillions of new money that could become around and in all of our pockets come newly cut and manufactured tight and right counted green papers. This is in and of the world's ideas and whatever is in the schools of these hard and the "knocked life" into the bandits of the new order of the ages in the costs and the official guides of the new order of the ages. These are in and of the official and rebellious peoples in the same natures of the games of life as me.

These are all alone and is inside the ways of the actions of man and in the natural ways in the worlds and in the life's ways that is towards the life of the beginnings of mine that are about the teachings of these certain values and in the strongly developed individuals that can set the moral standard for world war can be with world peace. These are of the world wars and the world peaces and inside of the sole persons of the inexperienced man's guidebook and inside the outlines of the life of the wrong and the faith and these dumber experiences and inside the world of the fallen angels and the fallen demons of the Biblical examples of the many Scriptures comes in what comes towards the everyday in the outward faiths in man afterward in the games of the life of the fallen persons and inside the fallen man the buried treasure chest. This is from and for the lives in the chance and the necessity of the forgiven and forgotten world's treasures that are in the lights and the faiths of the living revelations that are like you are from what I have and will have helped experience and in this have shaped the world's eyes in the lights of the lens of every person and each and every individual. Let us learn how to adjust and focus the lens of the other person's light in this sense of the real individual's light that can shine on down on another and the other person in the room.

This is about and in the book of the story in "Revelations". This is for and from these brand new experiences, inside the life of the wars that are for the plagued realities of the man. This is from the new experiences in the realities of the strange and unusual realities of the choices and the thoughts in mankind. These are in colors. These are inside the colors. There are standard and there are neutral colors. Let this color be of peace.

Out of all of this is in themes of the paper's theme and in this I do to go to the places of the life within and therein where we there are each of us and of ourselves and of the spots that are the usual and unusually large inside life and in whereof in which I could go in life and in this efforts I choose a situation's angle the ways among the situations that are in life and in the life of the situations that are relevant in the life of mine comes the life of it all in the elite in the situations of us all.

I am in a sin nature and that in which I can experience and choose from one term to another term that is to seemingly surprising among the details to the life among the ways that are in the situations and for whatever are in the good of the good book's life or the Holy Bible and of the life therein and in and inside and in the details of the life's knowledgeable choices and in the finessing choices that are in the insides of the man's way of life a kind of example of the settings of the trap for the bear. These are in and of the man that God did pick.

I did not have to choose the details of the life of man and in these issues and in these insides that are in and from and of these solid rocks there are titles of man that can represent and qualify him. This is to become one with himself and in the businesses of the inventions that becomes from the source of the rocks and of these inspirations in rock sports and in that comes in to whatever are with me and is of and comes from the money and the principles and prejudice and the values of the whole system of the money and in with me what in cash values are the value of the direct and fully harmful world without God where there are some new things and other newer things.

The one whose ideals and ideas came true and an apart without and within the help of God comes in many different forms of the real and sacred life that can always have a downfall and we can help and always hoping and helping that are for the ideals of the practice of the gone finished set free the zillions of the sacred money and in my real United States dollar bills there is for the life and for the life of us all is in all. This is of the President of the "United States of America's" traditional values and the sprawling Medias in the half and indeed input among the roaches of man.

This is from the roundabout and the entire way that is in mine and is in others and is in the contexts of the zillions of dollars from me to you to the government. This is all and always the part of the United States dollar bill that no one wants to talk about and in this is worth it all of doing it all in life and into these lives of these other peoples. Coming from what in what are in whatever are in all of what are in all of the damnation there are all of the real and the behavior in the real dollars and cents of the United States' Constitution and of the treasury there is a United State's dollar bill and is a God. In God we trust is an independently and upon the US Treasury's mottos the notes and the bills of it all.

These are and are of whatever seems like into the water is into the coming of all that are inside the fire and from a very little and alive furniture store and always in and towards the little things of the becoming in little of all that is in whatever is in my ever-present life in my current life that is in that there are hopefuls and sides to the sides and the order to represent in the order of America's capital comes the United States of America's very own and real chosen, Godly tradition.

There are in the very similar black inside and white outside of the places and in whatever does this therein comes blackness on the outside of the society of God. The snake is one of these species and spaces of the outcome of the outcomes of the altogether in what comes from and whatever comes towards in however way and in whatever way that become in life that are in these sacred things of the offered invitations or the dilemmas towards these facts of the information and in to information of the informative insurances that are; all towards the many different businesses and the forms and in it in the outcomes of the sources that are therein and thereof the places and that pictures of that which are in the money and are in the history of the details of the trustfulness of the conceptions of the life of all. This is inside of the month inside these arms of the history month of the inner "me" making inventions and these companies therein that are designing and building the business deals that are of the ideals and in that the concepts therein are chosen from the values.

There are whereof and in that there are to be selectively located many different forms and sources of inspirations of the dollars and sense in the whereabouts in the life of the money in the moneybags into the reality of the sources of the inspirational sources inside living and the chosen life therein that can complete the circle of life. There are the many different forms and techniques and the innate sources, which are within and of the inspiration of the very different sources of the man of the information of the man's outcome in living the right life for the good. This is, for together on the end of fiction. These are in what comes of the difference of sources that can control our world and in the resources there are different sources that are in different formations of the inspiration of the ways of man. The world's images in the shells of the occupying locations across the nation can become from what is from the source of the strength of the different location in the senses. This is and is in the differences that are in and are inside the very and very different realms of the calmness of mankind and the stables.

We are from that which we are of and are of these very sacred images and in the zillions in and of these sacred and entirety monetary means of the world to cast the images and of the countries that becomes these zillions of dollars inside the sake in the sense of the scene of these different locations.

They are always in and of the sacred and the main total life's essences and condemnations into these realms of these inner realms inside the money of God and of the very first hottest spots in the history of the money of the world. This is all about the money the money system and the yoke on the yard of the dog's name hair is fleece. This is about and of the money system of God. This is of the magic of the dog's name. This is about the "Cruz" dog for the "Cruising for a Bruising". This is in and of the dog's love. I had a friend who named his dog this name. He used it as a pun. This represents, man's best friend, in the greater scheme of things: the dog. Money is the man's best friend in the business world. That is why it is aforementioned here.

We are from whatever is inside of and of the whereabouts of whereof and where we were about to go and in to the spirits of the bodies and the souls and in the money and in the end it nothing else matters? These are foremost and formally into the ways toward the rightful inventions because these all can eventually go where the other inventions go: in the rightful places wherein the zillions.

The hidden soul of the business world can set you free and can set us over freedom's victory and over death's accolades and over ourselves. There are money and things that are influential and life-changing that can suspend or can reenact to the political issues and the principles of all of the modern day of the sense of modern man. In this zillion dollar world there is of the zillions of dollars that are completed after the ideas inside of all in the messages of these callings that can come of the issues and the memories that can become one by the words of the inside for the mainly historic and philosophic dilemma and the issues of the modern day man that can escape from us all. He was in the pictures that can become of whatever is in these same senses of the history in the individual masses of the individual world's views. From the foremost reality and further into the mainly and the mostly sought of dilemmas in the real and calm and stress-related behavior that is from and for the pits of mankind. These are in the associated groups or of the companies that are in these real and abusive the brand new and newer in format "New World Order". This is from the real and innate stress-related and the strain-related new conditions of the newest world of the good that the entirety of the world that is about the doing and helping of the others that are about and in also helping. These are from and are in these inside ways that are to telling and to seeing of these ways of the directions inside of the sane dictations and what is innately constructions and construction in the ways of relating to these forms and in who comes and in who is related to these constructions of the guidebooks and of the persuasions and the principalities inside of my new and old businesses that are the new and more improved related materials to all the sources of inspiration in these days of the modern day of mans that have been all a scapegoat of modernity and of what I like to have called and can have wanted all that could have been "all" and the "liked to call" the "scapegoat of modernity" in the fictions of the endings and the creations in the businesses of mine. This is of and about any of any of these senses and in the fire of these and there is the very modern scapegoat of modernity and the good scale for on the "modern day man". He is about the scapegoat. This is of the modernity. This is in how and in of he gets away and releases himself from the modern day man.

Coming by and from the first person's company experiences or in the angel's experiences in the companies that and set and of the very own charts and graphs and the figures therein and there comes out of the good experiences of businesses and the dough come the police and these donuts that are alive and well in the police officer's belly throughout the zillions in the United States currency of the marked dollar bills.

There must have been or is there a way, which is about, and to be at a rat race: for man. This is a rat race that is largely based on the abilities of the modern day man's race; whom is the briefly obvious scapegoat of modernity that means that in this there are no hopes.

This is all about the "ex". And of in this the countries of America however in he has to fully have towards all are to be what are the reality the reality of the known in what is as money does not leave the world ever but does any of ourselves towards or towards in this life in the dreams and associations of the associated people and from all of this leaving the dreams of mankind there are the mainly-known and "occupied" building. We must all try and become one with the images and traditions of the modern man?

In all of this becomes of and inside of us all not that is of us and but only the sidelines sidewalks and sideswipes of the roads are in the essences of man that are alive and are on the top in and of the condominiums of my life.

If all of this does not work inside these goods and for these only working places that are in the good and of these good things that are now of and in these good sides and good things of victims and inside of the places of the romance of the mans inside of these nomadic domes and the virtues and of mankind comes the colossal and inside the zillions of the world's money; and inside of the world is inside fiction.

This could not ever become what is about and inside of whatever are towards the man and into his businesses on the delay in the invention days. One comes of the destiny or of the lives within and wherein the moments of the seek and of the destroy method that comes through the traffic codes of the triple-x and inside of the circles therein of the clubs and inside these certain drug-related roads whereof there still stood what is inside of time and still this is inside on what still are in times that are needed in close to the spectrum of the choices of time. These ways that are of the living conditions and to the ways of these nomadic conditions are of this all in this wartime endeavors where there are none of that in whatever are in the inside of the days in the lives of man in the hopes of man and inside damnation. There is not an example of nothing and alone zillions?

And in all of this there still is and are therefore the mainly and mostly closed businesses and in the inventions of what made total sense to me and to man and in the whatever can make sense in the world dough is in the traffic record's situations in the life in man wherein one and then there becomes another one. This is from and of the zillions of that one's interest that must become in one's living conditions that are closely inside of these living lives of the zillions of the currencies of these zillions of the dollar babies of the modern man's living poverty in challenges and successes in the money system. In the cash babies with the old money and there in the living rooms of the houses and in the homes where we are that way that we are invested in and are living inside of today for and how we are all ready to live ourselves inside the conditions of war. Are the conditions then able and bodied and the conditions in the able conditions ready to be approved? Are we able of making zillions? In and of the modern day living of the modern man's dilemma in life of how is someone able to be put in the game that are the successes is the failures and are the dilemmas in these outcomes of and in mankind.

What does it mean to be reconciled? Do we have to talk and talk about making zillions? Is this impossible. In the government are where we can make all of our zillions that are ready and capable of being made.

Why do we need zillions in the Federal Reserve Bank of the United States of America's justice and temperance league? To pay off this national debt.

This is to own the world.

America should do this.

We have waited for long enough of time!

These business worlds are into the watches, of the world? He can become whatever becomes in what is in who lives inside of the conditions in the sense of the record of the "Guinness Book of World Records" that was about money. These are especially the money paychecks and secretive and hidden and sacred royalties. This is inside of these sacred and free royalties. This is of and in the world.

These are a faction of a percent in life and a very "far off" places way was all good in the times of need: where we are all in good. The money was for the businesses and of the money inventions and in the real 'first-person started it kind of the certain kind of and in this the appeal was in there where there was a thought-induced pleasure done in this manner and type of experience and in the drug's induced and freedom induced totally extorted and harsh drugs induced reality there are wherein the totalities of that which we have seen and yet in the above that have studied monies and have seen above in this issues of money and in the below part from the money's influences on society and in the spending of the values of the real man- money's power trick a life.

These tales inside of whoever has spoken to us and in and of ourselves wherein there has been and are the location of the money system's locations and places and into all of its businesses there is the business and there are the businesses that are in inventing!

And all of this is alone and into these shadows and the real darkness comes the reality of the places where these businesses of the new world order's reality of the locations of all come home to the endlessness of the tiredness that become in one. In the locations of the places where the business companies exist there are the locations in the Dallas Texas's region of the world. These are from Dallas Texas and other locations in the ones of and in itself in Christ and in the places of the domes and in the reality of the forests comes the man come home from the world war.

There are both sets of the location that are in these places and where the businesses and places and pleasures are and the inventions and in whatever is in these come inner placements. These are where the sacred and that are places these around the globe onside of the growths of growing and in that was in the businesses of the unusual that are in whatever is in somewhat unusual in the places in where we can and are become of the growing. These are and are for the length of all of these times wherein that of itself takes towards a growing of the trees inside three days. This is of business and is in the inventions of all of the business soil. This is about and for the soil. This lets the businesses growing larger into the principles and the made-up inventions inside of us all.

There are of these locations and in then these were about God. These are in the certain businesses places where there are the valuables and in that are inside and in and inside of the callings becomes and came the offered inside step into the sources of these calling in their inspirations that are from and in these sources that are in and inside the lands of for ever in time. The days of the time where of these countries and these trees where we and each of us or all of which are location wise in the eventful youth in all of the very and entire successes that are fully capable and ready inside these ready walls that if whatever is in these lives there are also lives that are in life. These actually do not pertain to business. This is if not very well.

These are of mankind's images and in whatever are in the life of mine is from there many of the world and in that are that which are of whenever they are off of and in and where this is is inside the money of if there is the magic of the sole decisions inside of man: 1. The first off is God 2. Inside the beginning and second is God; throughout Jesus Christ 3. The insides of the starting of the country's treasures of the entirety of the entirety of the lives of many are from the insides of the God of the all of trouble.

These are of mine that are about the mine and where it goes. The directions are about the money and where the money goes and when the money listed that is on growth chart of the main of the economy and the secondhand look at what it takes to overdo the control in the whole world with successes and in the life of the failures to the ending there has always been around the dice the main of the ways that we move into the mirror images even in images.

This book is about the money. This is from the profits and the gains of the economy to these value books. There are money from and in the mirrors of the nonprofits and are from the values in man and is in the first-off found and sources and the follow us through and the junctures of the man in the future and the past of the time's goals and the real and all-time functioning about the God of man and about the sourcing that are sure and steady with the man and the one in the futures of the lives of the man in the mostly unknowingly but very abundant show that must go on. In oneself and in what should always continue on the issues and problems are cast forth inwardly going towards the economic good of the magic. There are destined the magic problems and an even so to insults that are made sense of for good in the economy inside of the good that is of trust in money and for treasures in man and for reaches in society. There are magic ways that in return show off and should always see and think from the "good" men and also women towards the products of our seeing to where we do not know.

These are those that are around and inside the life of gaining whatever is lost that can be treasured as whatever are sense in whom are in goodness that are to have all fell responsible for the news of the country and the world's growing economy inside the falseness of it all in senses that go around the world! They then go to flourish and into the loss and to gain appeal and powers among the other people's victory of the gaining of the country's real and first-off seat that in what is where all can with all of us going forth go into all that becomes towards what is all inside functioning within the economy.

These can become in life what it is to see the first off of the faithful ideological ways and into a source the very trustful opportunities to volunteer inside of the opportunities of the faith of God to grow bigger and inside the jobs and these faiths of man and inside Christ then lastly take advantage of the peoples in and of the end.

In all of this virtues and of these new world order members and these losses inwardly to them are always in the end trustfully and happy towards the end. This is all from the sources of the victories and the offset of the adventures of sexual encountering and having a lot of all the deeply-rooted kinds of the individuals in sex and inward into the sources of cash-money inside the steady flow of the economy. This is about the steady flow of the economy. It is all about the steady ebbing and flowing of the sexes in the diagram of the sexes and in however they both come together. This is from the flow of money to the production of the cash.

These are the people with the others that are of the realms of living to the last one's off-duty and "off-line" sources and products from the sources of inspirations and the flourishes off the map in whatever is of the men and of these women comes inside and in and about theirs and inside of theirs shoes within these occupancies alone and the second alert inside these very alert businesses and to the businesses inwardly there are the thoughts that are of and are inside the many places of the inventions and these inventions are the sources of inspiration into the zillions of dollars of reality. The growth into these harshest realities and always into what is coming from these triumphs that are the most fun business places come around the whole world. This came from whatever are in the world in what we have that becomes inside in all.

These are of the known approach to victories and came from the individualistic approach in the firsthand. These first appearances come out and to grow into bigger ones greatly magnifying the source of the originality in greatness. These are in the greater occupations of these lives that come around inside of oneself and he that have values. These occupations of life we cannot just spend on a time and an ending place in these hidden and the realistic lives.

These men and their occupations are in what people comes from where we want to direct the landed product. These are if the sales come to the adrift in these sands. Sands of time and one and ourselves inside of the Garden of Eden become after the falls in man and of the greatness offered in the lives and inside and of these many deaths that come apart and together and alone in life all survives in this life where we can form. Coming from all the thought and the mostly infamous of the thoughts that is needed to survive become man and its images there are of man that are survival throughout businesses and inside the inventions throughout the times to spare and these times to adjust to the one who is man's allies inside these forces. This is into the real world's dilemmas and inside of these occupational successes of these secret shoes and in and of the secret pairs inside where are gone inside we are gone.

There are the shoes of paradise that are in the Garden of Eden that those shoes are in shoes. There is and are inside these shoes. These are of and in the substance. This is in the Dinosaur and the eggs that are of the shoes within and of how they all fit if they fit the best. These are for the wearing of the rightful shoes if that are and is if they fit right and if they fit on your feet's design. These living things are all of and about these rightful and correct fits of shoes. This is in the form fit.

These gradual business deals and of its appealing values and for thereof one in once more inside all of these issues and the financial gaining of the life of the ways that are through truth in lies and inside lies and toward lies becomes matter and the processes in and of these businesses that are in magic. There are the ways in the realness into the business truth and of these very real and very faithful approaches towards the location in man's endeavors and in man there is lives and there is sexual approaches.

These are the victories of the ghost of the world in whatever has understood in the gain of us and inwardly into without us how into all that we have into whichever is in that which is in the lives of these people and the individuals in these faiths.

From whatever becomes one of this are very understood and very well grounded in understood theories in the faiths of these sources of the economy that are in the economy in well-grounded theories that are in the ways and in the faith of man. This is from the game and of these prophets that become in the games of life. These are in the false economy and are of these games of life. These are of and in the games and in the awareness of the economy that is lies within man. These are of and in the realms of the goodness in mankind. The worlds are and are inside the ways of the worldly in man. To buy about inventions and to sell the offers to the other person of the games into these lives of the man from the world and into the cubbyhole there are in whatever comes a source of direction and a perfect place in diction that can uphold and that can upkeep the origins of the soul inwardly into the foot's resting spot inside the sock. The new world order can become, and in all theories and hypotheses, should be what is one's resting spots onside the journey throughout these business worlds of the forceful type of shoes. This is in the methods of the thought in the order offered the organized thinking individuals in the schools of the University of Oxford. This is inside of whereof I cannot just mold but I cannot just also heal the toe of the feet. The forceful occupations are not in love within the world. These are the occupations of the justices of the world.

These are from and are for these teams of finance to create equality. The world's teams are for the improvement for the quality inside life and through paying for games of the economy. These are the sole and originators of this necessity in the future minds.

The issues wherein and about the real game of the paper chase, there are always been, and have always been a "God of All". This is from the inventions lifestyle inside the games and the businesses of the "new world order" and in that that can become in whatever is from the money games can become this quintessential "life". The world's ownership democracy is first then discovery by whatever is all about there styles and the innate and natural guidance of the money-system and the situations and from the lifestyles comes inside these spending in money of these times in the need of man those enduring qualities. There are of the 'money-related' occupation is that invention-oriented quality by the events coming from those in businesses and inside the products of game that have been "hand-in-hand" looking for the locations of the worldly substances and of the games of the abuse of the substances in cash that are in "cold-hard currencies" that are from becoming of whatever are inside the chosen lives that are from the issuing of the systems of the currencies and of cold and hard "cash-flow" in the mainly quixotic substances of the same games inside the games of my lifetime's money inside the occupations of mankind. There are and is always about God there inside on the insides of their game-profits of the gaining of the life of mine where people are discovered. In the stories of the disgruntled lands to the discovery of it all behaved with the behaviors out into ways in line controlling the factors of the money system and from in and from where of it all goes into the ending. This is not about to enter and go into whatever is in the money system's game and buying power. This is from the trials and tribulations of one mankind's values and another's purchases way beyond the cash buying systems. This is of and in the values of the entrance into the gates that is of the power of the purchasing of the values that are of mankind.

The money and the actions in whatever in one's lives and these deaths can speak louder than the "current words" of 'cash-flow'. These can equally and rightfully make sense toward you in the money system. The monies in the "insides" of the game of the "new world order" are about the real money inside these values of God.

These are the valuable businesses and the promoted inventions that are inside the money industry and come from the sole monetary values and into the original cash-flow ideas of the profit and currency inside money of there real life and the directions in the love of the money currency in life. This is in the chances for the evil inside the world inwardly and inside and of the life and about the immortal sacred lives those in the currency of the real man's motto and deliverance into these systems of the real good prodigious outcomes and the current students of the industry of the desires of man and from the "money game" there are that people that are studious and student's values. They are rich and poor in the bigger and better than life complete and real outcomes into the money and cash of the economy. These are compared to all from whatever is inside and becomes into the depths of what this is and that which is into whatever and forever comes in inside whatever can than that what can hatch in the eyes of the chicken laying the eggs and the eggs hatching whether it is all by itself. The money system is in the cash system's flow.

These are the models and prototypes for the up keeping and real "inventions and businesses" that are from all of life's games. There are also the money solutions and the tides of whatever that are in which complete these cares inside these endeavors.

These are in the outcomes of the promoted money that becomes from the "Holy Ghost" that are from goodness that cares for which are from the "Holy Trinity". These are and are in the goodness of God. These are in the context and contents of God. He is in the inventions and business of the world's attribute of God's children.

The real God or the "Holy Spirit" lives inside of me: for whomever forever and forever is in the closed closet of mine. This 'three-in-one-persons' is from what that appears and comes of the "Holy Trinity" that is in the "holy spirit" comes God. This is from decisions and inside the values and the business money that is "about the coveted" holiest of the 'holy trinity'.

Money or the family of God's life is inside in money. The inventions are that if these whole world endeavors and in the whole-wide-world works in hands at first and the "second hands" is if we see what we are for working in the "new world order" that becomes towards these reality and business' term: then there then is the valuable "God". There is whatever are and is offered of my only one invention towards another one's businesses in the persons' invention's that are; towards the making of the "make sense". These are from the directions and in the sole and whole wide world of "God". These are and are about from the victims of the "good" and from these lives and in the captive victims of whatever comes from God are of what is 'God'. There becomes money and in whatever are in "Jesus Christ" and God comes in the holy and sacred blessing of the "Trinity". He is of values and opportune victims and the notions in businesses and at the goodness that are inside the lives in mine and are in the "goodness" in the right values of the mortal of the immortalities of the God. This is from all from the Holy Spirit and the money in the world.

There are and is of and about one man's one's valuable people's viabilities that are from the rock of God's world. This is in "the businesses of man" and in that is in the man of the whole 'new world order'. These are the cash and the money that are in "the non-negotiable terms" that is from one man's virtues toward another human man's "victories" to another human "man" whatever is for the greatness and goodness victory of God. This is in the sole options and the enclosures of one man into another man's hero in "the heroic story" of the lives in the ending inside money. There is of cash-flow and mucho money that are deep inside of God's virtues and of these endings in man's virtues the principles and valuables of the virtues of man. Where we are closed captive is where we remain forever. This is of "Jesus Christ".

These issues that are in the "new world order" and are in the life of money and in this essence in which are in this and that life that becomes of which is in this story and are always in these monetary values and the necessity inside of "cash-flow" and in this ready monetary situation comes the bartering. These are of this situation and in from the heart of cash come in whatever is this inside cash flows of the economy.

Money and the monetarily gaining cashes and formats that appears to be one of the money games is these games of the money gain or the mainly loss. The loss of this is equally in and old and of these truthfulness and the lies therein and thereof the cash industry should will and might not ability-wise be able to do in money terms. There is the trustfulness of the worldly person's members and in this money world there are a lot of money loaners that can work for all. This becomes one and the respectfulness of its very real and own dimensions of the ending of this all might become pared with one another in the end.

These are forever from, and the entire passions of God. This comes inside of the whole world's wide world and the brand new "new world order" in where the "Antichrist" or the "World Leader" known as the "man" is the brand new way of the "new world order". This is about the funny sides in the times that we had together and are spent apart or in these great times together there have been an "Antichrist" that sees and the occupations in the entire world of God's whole entire world of fun. This is about the businesses and the inventions.

There is one person who comes cleaner in the inside businesses inside the faction of these people in the "new world order". These are from the ways of the entire world. There is and are the essences and condemnations in the life of mine. There are demons and angels in the movie of the, "Wizard of Oz". There are and is this business in the 'new world order' of "man". The action of the good man is from the long and hard hours of operation? This is from in the truth and the values and the respects of God. This is in these one truth and the essences in the experiences of the money. And in the inside of God becomes Jesus Christ. God is in these values and of these offered lives and sacredly in these solely outcomes of the singularly of the single business world of God.

And of the whole world and inside the world one part's occupations in businesses becomes one sole and wholly responsible plans of God and into and inside of the plans of God comes these inventions and the businesses' values that are God's.

There are more than just the businesses that come from the inventions and from whatever is from God. This is of which are of the businesses and are inside the parts of the one's business that is one's becoming from the plans of the God's values becoming one in the "new world order" or the "new order of the ages". The traditions in the businesses plans that are still towards victory in the daily values of the United States. There is equality in the second victory and in these second one's chances are from our Jesus Christ. What ever is in what becomes of one's victories over the businesses of the world is Riley Miller. This is from mainly impossible charts and graphs in the business world's outcomes. So toward the invention's profitable endeavors and the charts of the profits comes the businesses' endeavor. The worlds of businesses that are what is financed are much more extreme and utmost in this question of whether or not we should do business with you altogether. The roads are the longer lasting products and the products are in the inventions of mine. With the minds ingenious inside and in the world of businesses came of the game of life. These are from the businesses of the "new world order" and in these businesses and inventing and production of the money in people's vast accounts of the business world's real money reserve and in these inventions of mine that there are many that are equally paid become that are in equal payment.

Alone and in and from a person to another one person there comes money from God. To the certain businesses and all into the "new world order" of the other businesses became a large value. The values and resources of the man are from the one that is big. This comes down to another business with another name "New Order of the Ages".

It is in him who has the responsible parties' parts in whatever becomes in the ways of more than the lives but in life there are more than only one of the world's businesses. The ways of man and in life are from the days and the trials and the nighttime where there is business. The prodigy of these businesses of these businesses inside the businessman; there comes God.

I think that can become inventions is alone that we can buy. The one and sole business is about the buy. There has and are more businesses than that are from one and another into the values of the businesses. This is the holistic and values of the businesses that one become.

This is the one in whatever are in the greater and moreover one's values that became alone in and from these inwardly and outer sacred tales and in the insides of all that are whatever are of these victories of lives comes God. The Holy Ghost and inside of God becomes ones into the real victories of the real "God Almighty" and the only "Victor" me for the days and lives of the inner and sacred and from the inside of the God of All has the deals inside the inventions of the games that are always for the treasures from the offered dollars into these values of the days of my lives forever in my inner lives and inner beings there becomes one God. There are the plans that are within the hidden societies in what are located within the plans into the business endeavors of mine that can and that have been secret and hidden until now. The plans and mine are to go into the reality of the world that has the real working out intelligences within the idealistic me" inside and of the deals and in the real businesses and the progresses therein the world that are and would cause harm to someone and can not true this with clean us out and make us bigger as a newer nation that therein under these stars and the capitalists under the communists that are under the God's living values of that the games is of the freedoms off the values of the reasons of the principles of us all in this United States. This is of and in His very own biggest time into the man's endeavors wherein the ways of the nationalistic and unitary values of the nationalistic treasures and values of God into the righteousness of man. The beautiful victories and the beautiful victory are of God.

Greater than this and more than this are and is in the mainly ideas in treasures and the businesses' principles and offered in the "new order of the ages" is the truthful values inside the "greater" opportunities that are inside of mankind that we are within the God's with us all. These are from the United States of America and inside of values and the opportunities there lies the Holy Spirit's reality of these inner and outer lives of the hidden America and inside from and of these real lives and the sacred issues of the myths and the truthfulness therein are within our sacred mankind.

These are of the greater mankind's agenda's issues within the games that operates in life's greater occupations under the whole values and from and in this greater issues of ideal is inside the nations of these states in these sacred and hidden ideologies and the legislatures of the opportunities and within this to caste out the votes of the "American traditions" and under the flags and in this country the "US Constitution" of wherein there is in ours is the "United States Constitution" and the "Bill of Rights" of this mankind.

These Constitutions and in this inner sanction and sanctity that are of the sacredness of these political lives and in this business endeavor where we are each person a life to always "live with and do" and in this direction of independence the reality of the world and inwardly from the inner soles and these mainly the games, of the knowingly God's values and issues and in this issues of the bringing forth of lives are whatever inside of whatever are what comes and is shown in us. This is from and come to forth the lives of all. The invention's values and in this effort of these efforts in this treasured life values of mine comes the real God.

He is in whatever becomes in these values in with and inside of one only my very good and valued God's issue that should in whatever I can become have that which is of these principles in whatever comes from the coming of the ages that is in man. These are that which are good and goodness of the ancient and sacred of these businesses are in all that have on the values and the opportunities that have made us within our own difficulties and in these differences that has made us all free becomes the democracy of the nations and the progresses of man that is alive and well in us.

These are under the "traditions and values" of the mainly and solely and frankly in the learned life in the life of all that are inside and into these principles and in this inner thought the inner values of the nation's deals and the economics of the businesses of man and of mine offered in the traditions of mankind. In the sole representations in the life of the living in and for the sole and soulful duties and respectfulness whatever are these are thereof these insides of the God of the buried treasure.

And into the hallmark of zillions of dollars and in all of these educated learning of mine and in the God's tomorrow comes to the writings of the each and to the day and in to yesterday and in to the future stillness of life are greatnesses. These are in the comings of the God from the Trinity and of these Godly attributes and in and of however the insides into the factors in the zillions of the world in God and in the insides of is whatever becomes God's meaningful zillions is inside of these insides in the mankind of the mankind of man's very meaningful inventions and in the progresses in the lifetimes of mine is inside these blessings of God. The world equally and inside reality becomes after man. This is in the Christian tradition of the salutations and these philosophies of the inner sales of these inwardly lives and these life's values. These are in and of the values of mankind.

These are of these orientated orientations inside thinking that are all inside us all within and of the God of all things that come true and can become whatever becomes true inside the living tales and values of; man's times of values in the hidden secretive tales in mine. This is about the values the adventures and inside and in the of of these are "Garden of Eden". This is in itself and in this came from the tales from these issues and the philosophies of whatever is inside halls and into passageways and is into these values and insides of mankind. This is in the values of God. These hidden inventions and sacred businesses and then these clients of man that are within us all become of that which are in the light of the Christianity and the Gospel and the traditions of the secrets and inside these are the learned Scriptures of God's mankind's values. We are that which are inside and offered in these heroes of tomorrow where the ideas and the inventions can and does become whatever is better to us and inside these ideals and hidden lives is whatever can and does, become what goes. This is whatever can goes towards the little man. He is in the big man of the Scriptural ideas and fundamental philosophies of the God of All. These hidden values and secretive methodologies are of and in the traditions of God.

This is that which is whatever lasts the longest times and can become one whose plays become into these realities and the important roles of life therein the necessities of the God inside us all and of the man and of the mankind; come undone. This becomes one in one and each and every one of these endeavors that are within these lives that are from the deep within these insides of the Godliness of the man and in God. He is and isn't inside each and every man but he comes apart and comes alive inside the inventions of mankind. He has and been making born lives and then has mastered and has found in God the locations and these workers. This is about the life into manliness and into these realms of Godliness in man. These are in the God of all.

These are from the shortcomings and are from the brand new issues that are within and formed within life that are successful and within games that are in the brand new formats of the possibilities of fictions and in that these newer products that becomes in God in all of these the products of these issues that are from these games in life are successes. I met the most successful man and he was of all a bum. He became in God. He was inside God. And He is in the images of God. This person could have been me. The reasons for why I tell all of you this is because I am of a God. He is in fiction. God is in these Bibles. Jesus Christ is inside these Bibles. Holy Spirit is inside the Bibles. We are inside the real big times and the lives of ours. These are to set the standards. These are from the whole of Godliness.

This was from whatever he has money to spend on and in whomever he has had with him on whatever there becomes and are inside of the reality of the man to the lives that are offered in him while the clients' real big times of successes of the mankind's virtues are times. This is in the businesses and the clients.

These are from the money the game and the powers that can be whatever are what come from the real big dog's natural businesses: Riley Parker Miller. He comes from whatever is of the real world's goodness's and of these insides of every oneself and from that which becomes from these Godly insides comes into life and into the sale in these intelligences and these source and driven reality and inspirations that are in one's driven quantities for life and death and for what can become from what comes from the source of the bigger endeavors and inside the very treasures of the driven deals are the costs from these issues and the very many different forms and these primary factors and into the new world order of these secondary sources of inspiration are all that have and are of and in these inspirational matters and from and this in life there are these inventions and the endeavors in businesses in the worlds of fun. This is about and from these businesses. This is about and of the operational procedures in mankind. These are of and from the Medias progress. The sole is from the capital of man and inside the reason of man comes the opportunity and in the ability of God.

This is inventions and the within idea: the inner and outer real McCoy of not just of one of oneself and his God that is in times and the business natures with me comes the drank wines of the Garden of Eden whereof we have all evolved and have changed into the lives and the inner tales of the happenings and the traditionally known issues and items that are about how time has forgot about God. Yet I dedicate this towards the real me; the, indestructible me that is not in just about science, but is about the many world's orders. This is about the game. This is in all levels that are happened to me.

There are theories in what really occurs and in whatever has lifetimes and all has been produced equally and inside of life and in whatever I have become in these good promises and are from whatever is this world of thoughts inside and the very inner ideas that have had promises in that belief and inside that of is in oneself and towards that have the resources and the times inside the little times we needed to be solved in God; is Christ.

This is to create and to produce all of the newer products and in these driven realities and in the forceful inspirations that are inside the life of the lives and in the beginning, and inside to be of what are that which are inside God in fictions becomes God. These are from one's inside of whomever the games could become more like in one's issues and principles with that which are more and many more of these ideals and principles coming from the different opinions and these philosophies of life therein is the games and the little transitions in the difficulties of the game and the different sources within of knowledge and the inspirational teachings of the challenges in the God. This is in the intelligences of the good and bad and the successes in these good times the theories with in what are for the bigger time and of the knowledge with man that wins that is with the only noble requests and quests for all that is in mankind. This is of and in God.

This is the new beginning of all of the newer and more produced inside intelligences that are inside all products and brands and inside lives inside of whatever are the examples of a reality driven society; these strictly coded examples of the reality of the height of the many good examples and inside the intelligence of reality the greater example inside man that I can promote and solve in itself in order in terms in communication to find and to build an empire with intelligence of good materials of the time being and into the world of fun and promotion of the greater times in what these better and more improved intelligences and communities of mankind's miracles and wonders and signs of materials that are built with the product's realm and occupying histories wherein the real new man's knowledge. These are about and of the modern man's products and businesses. These are from trust and compromise of good and new relationships that are with man. He is with the man of inventions and the new world order of man's relationship with fictions.

These are in what makes reality a newer and more real phenomenon. This is from and in the challenges of the new races in man. This is from that which can come true. This is only to you. And always this is from fiction. This is about the fictions and the realities. These are from the marches and races of mankind inside and in these illusions that fact can break and newer phenomena can really one becomes with whatever exists in the world. This is what does this for money in the world of essences and condemnations and books that have all and in this faction of the world's money there are everyday people and in the countries that we are inside of there are everyone's lives and these fictions and knowledge realities that we buy into and we do not even know why the real world does all of these in fictions and in the realities that are lived inside of forever inside the endings of these days' successes that are in time and is new time.

These are in the end. These are having and are about the God of it all inside the traditions of the Lamb's property to own the: "Garden of Eden". This is of the inventions of mine. These are of and into the coming of man and are in the return of God in the laws that are inside of God's property and in this the real God of all and the Son of God and the real and inner properties that we've explained is inside the nutrients of God. These are in His looks. The first Garden of Eden fell of nature in nature and by nature; in the beginning in man. These are, for God's providences.

We hope and see and know that this very own mold is about math and succumbs towards all of the fictions in God. This is whatever and why ever we are separated in this distaste and these ways of the worlds of liking and this is what is separated from us that are both for and about the very and much truer ways of the excellence in man. This is coming from the newer and more in the se ways of God that are "newer and more fascinating" within the God of knowledge and in the Godliness of excellences in the worldly and wide ways of the man and God.

God is this creator and example in the living traditions of our much more and in this more inner sanction of the inner world there are codes and languages and the tried and more of the experienced reality that we have all been throughout in this true nation with the codes and the languages this can not make sense to in these fictions and the reality of God.

In all of this there would be a person or one whose inner lives can pretend to create the new world order's issues. These inside life can take and see more of whatever is from some friendships and the connections therein to succeed with all things in success and in the new world order's frameworks of man's becoming inside and into these traditions of the space and time of man.

This is from and to the real world of Riley Miller. This is from and of the traditions and the guiding light of these future reoccurrences inside of the new world order and its becoming towards the little and bigger one and only and futures and inside the ownership of man's images and the kinds of these images that are inside and in all of man. These are in and for God. I am a Christian inventor and Godly entrepreneur within the all of God from these times and essences inside of the real spirits and beings of mankind from God and for sure towards God.

These is to coming into those who love us all and in each and offered to this everyone of us we will become oneself in order to understand the sales and the operations of all of mankind's images and likings in man. These are coming throughout the gateways of science fiction and technological devices in man. These are from the future coming and past history of man's triumph and successful endeavors and directions in mankind's future of progress towards the man and inside the liberty and independence of man a greater notion the successes of the vocations and invitations of man's issues. These are in the provinces of God. Where are the provinces of God? This is about and in the natures of primaries and secondary issues in life. These are from constructive criticism and the manipulated and thought-to beings inside of these; real Godlike and Godly natures of living and in the statutes in mankind of the progress and of the natural beings that choice of God.

1. New species of plants that are created. These are self-germinating plants that are these organic or self-fertilizing plants. Describes plant that "pollinates" itself with an organic and natural seed meaning that it can transfer pollen grains from the male structure of a plant to the female structure of a plant and fertilize it. This is from organic to natural seed. This creates an organic plant which becomes a natural plant.

They will have seeds in their insides that are organic that become natural over a period of time. They are self-germinating plants with organic or man made seeds that are made to be different new plants. These seeds are combined with other natural seeds. The plants will have seeds that can self-germinate. Organic plants which can be made in almost natural ways in life. These are made with seeds. These create new plant types. These are all in different areas of the world. These are made in labs.

This is used to describe a plant that is capable of pollinating itself. This means that it can transfer pollen grains from the male structure of a plant for example the anther to the female structure of a plant for example the stigma and fertilize it. They can be implanted into the ground across the world to let them grow. They are made in labs and the organic part of the plant is created. This is a natural way to create plants. They create an organic seed in a lab and then make it natural. √

2. A new device for anything that is a battery that attaches itself that can be charged. It can be charged from a satellite. It will revolutionize battery chargers. It's a charger that goes on the battery that makes the battery better. This charger is made to be in transition with the satellite in orbit. It can charge the battery from great lengths. It charges the battery from home or at the house. It can charge itself from the outsourcing from other satellites. It is for big or small things. √

3. This is a password card. It is a business card that is designed for school. The business card is not a sale card but a password card to get into the school. It is used. It is used to get into schools. √

4. A device used for stereos that can intercept messages from other individuals. It is a wave interceptor that can be used to talk through music. √

5. A locator that can be programmed to find anything. It goes on all types of phones because anything that is portable can be lost. These go on your car keys. It chirps or has a beep. It also has a timer on it to time the contraptions. √√

6. This is a three-way interceptor that is a radio that talks to people of the known world. It has a range through satellites. It is a company that develops these three-way interceptors that is a good option for all businesses. It is great for developing products of this natural nature. √

7. Instant message machine for portable purposes. It will have a buddy list of many options. It can be done on other Internet purposes or the one of the actual portable one. √

8. Cordless electronic server that can be plugged into the computer. This can be done with ease in the simple logistic of the computers. √

9. *This is a revitalizing drink for sports and medical reasons. It has every needed nutrient plus a new one that restores energy lost health. It is not a tonic but could work like one. It restores lost health to anyone in need. Athletes sick people hospitalized people will get a big kick out of this one. It will be in stores everywhere because it is good. It is the best thing for health that you can do to yourself. These Diseases are caused by insufficiency in laziness.

This drink will have all the proper ingredients like nutrient and anything else in the worlds. √

9. These are gel-surrounded shoes. This has the real surround gel. √

10. This is the go-system for cars. This is the invention of the hypersensitive driving system. √

11. Truthfully this is a company that designs things for closets. It is designed for closets to be painted as such. This closet is designed in a manner for the painting of the closet. √

12. The real system of thought producing societies that created propaganda. This is the promotion of ideas. √

13. A pedal system connected to one's suspension which makes the pedal go down when someone hits the brakes as well as hits something on the road. It also generates a nice effect for driving. √

14. It adjusts the speed of the car automatically with the type of road you're on in driving. As well as makes shocks adjust to the type of driving you're doing. √

15. A real go-button that will allow a person inside the vehicle to adjust the height of the suspension as well as the shock pressure is this invention. √

16. a control button in which will adjust the pressure of the shocks from very hard to very soft firm 'to' easy. √√√

18. Biodegradable nontoxic trash spray is this invention. √

19. Genes that can change to change body and mind forms. This will be revolutionary to say it in a word. The fruit like the body can also be done with this to produce much improved fruit. That is where it stops. Heck the Liger could be made. The genes from this could be made into a great thing for our planet. This is bigger growth and better taste etc. All produce of good engineering of the genetic type. √

20. An "ATM" card that can get thousands out of the bank with in one transaction. √

21. Translator that you can carry around and speak a language. It can be plugged into a cell phone or TV device or any other device. √

22. A new type of device that allows some type of communication under water. Under water communication pretty much walkie-talkie that is waterproof. This walkie-talkie is able to resist water. √

23. Love gene through understanding the molecular compounds of genetics. √

24. Laser gun for the armed forces all over the world. It can shoot extremely fast. It has more power than the regular. √

25. Objects that have talking features that can talk to you with real intelligence. √

26. An away message like smarter child that can be different personalities. √

27. New type of waves in which are generic in types of all kinds. This is new technology that is all kind of waves. This is sound digital for the cell phone and microwave as well as any other type of wave in one. Technologically sound and advanced with new types of research that will make it this way. It will be all these things plus more. It will be a great idea. This is combining all the waves into one generative wave. Generative means that it is a capability in or of producing something. √

28. A case that is for gasoline that will become extreme. This is safe as can be. √

29. Waterproof wrap that can be tapes for just about anything. √

30. A car coat paints that will never rust or get any sun damage or anything wrong with it. √

31. The brake strip goes on tires and reduces the brake speed. √

32. This tire traction for small traction heat deducing tires will allow them to go over anything it will be like a chain only much better on the tires. It can be put on for snow and cold weather. This is a very impressive substitute for chains on the tires. √

33. Media locator for TV remote controls that automatically finds the type of Television types for remotes. √

34. The producing of society. This produces societal influences on other men and women who like to gamble. It is the gambling world of promotion through video games. √

35. The product of the environment. This is a net-producing company that catches thought. It is in nature that this world is not good enough for. It promotes nature that way. √

36. This is the drinking pill. A pill designed for drunkenness which takes away the dizziness vomiting and sobers up. If person is too drunk causes mild vomiting. √

37. A pill that has the same chemicals as alcohol that can be induced into the system. This protects you from harm. √

38. This is an ice skate shoe that skates on ice. This skate shoe is the most projected object in history. If you catch my drift. √

39. Make your own bumper stickers? √

40. Car screens that shows where remote cars are coming in which direction as well as very cool technology showing roads. Screen on board cars. √

41. The perfect balance knife is equal in proportion with blade and handle. √

42. DVD that has movie music on it. Very cool device that can be bought with the DVD in a store. It is in the DVD movie. This is extremely successful invention that this is. This will be for sure. For people who like to enjoy music soundtracks as well as movies. These are two in one device.

*43. See through tape that is permanent. It can be removed by putting gel on the back of it. Very cool idea and will be successful. It can be very thick or very thin depending on what use it is for. Also it can be in different colors but see-through is the most common for this type of invention or should be and will. √

44. These are for real "sock shoes". These socks can be slipped on like a shoe. They will have relaxation to them which is their main ally. These socks will go on your feet like a shoe. √

45. Legal drugs. Heighten the senses but do not do anything bad. They can provide simple heightened euphoria no antidepressants necessary anymore! √

46. These are the plastic bags. The plastic grocery bag that does not bend or corrupt in heat or break will project these. √

47. Disposable oven slips that put on hand like oven mitt very useful and good. They are not hot and do not burn hand. No more obnoxiousness. Easy to use and comes with many different ones. Very useful. √

48. Contact lenses that do not irritate. They are made of better more sensitive plastic that will work wonders in the area of eye sensitivity. This is a good product. √

49. Garden hose that can bend easily but not cut off water flow very flexible. This is a new innovation exclusively for this idea. √

50. The mitts that will never become hot for the oven. This is very inexpensive technology. It is an innovation for the kitchen housing. √

51. The car dash that this is will show becomes exactly whatever the right weather is that which will happen when it happens. √

52. Car stereo that can adjust to users' preferences. It will have various features like most played and most rated best songs for movie soundtracks best songs for relaxation and the best for fast driving. This is the best in companies. √

53. These are scanners for your house. These are very useful and go to your house. These are built on a rock solid. √

54. Alarm that locks all doors with second lock and locks steering wheel automatically when goes off. Very useful and intuitive system of alarms. Will work well to eliminate people trying to steal or "borrow" car. √

55. A car system that is designed to talk to other cars in the area. It will be a system like a speaker but will be different. It can talk to other cars in front behind or in a radius of about 30 feet to thirty miles depending on the setting that one wants. √

56. A new wave receiver for cars that will help cell phone connection be put on top of the car. It will be for cell phones exclusively. Satellite dish similar in usage and form technology. Much smaller and sleeker. √

57. Cell phone receptor for other communication devices. Receptor that can pick up talking from cell phones. It will work well in other countries other than US or the officers of the law in the US. √

58. A small ball that can expand into a spider that has remote control legs. √

59. A bit for a computer that can be taken out easily and be put into other computers. Very easy to access and easy to handle. It is like the microchip except it stores all the stuff in the computer. It is used for giving other people yours. √

60. This is a remote control battery charger. It then works from over many many miles. It is a very cool smart and sleek. Very smart because of the technology involved in making it for people is it. It will be able to charge batteries from very far with a signal like a cell phone. √

61. Engine that has an internal charger for battery. These batteries is charged from three locations the engine the belt and the starter. The starter is hooked up to it and it keeps on putting the electricity from the car to the battery's charger. Then the charger is magnified by ten times until the battery is charged by having a belt that charges the charger. √

62. Turbo electric power. Much stronger than normal electricity. Uses much more power with more efficient use. Has faster electric travel like the "LAN" cord yet similar in form to normal electricity. Very efficient usage code. Code will be very similar to electric current except much further along. Technology is the best ally for this beast. It will consume power from a generator that is very powerful. It will be in houses all over the world and buildings. It will use modem-like tech. to use electricity in the form of waves. This is the new wave of technology. Electric current pure and simple the current of the way of the world. √

63. This is the satellite movie network. Many different titles of movies to choose from in your home or anywhere with a television to the subscription. Can pick any and watch. √

64. This is the electronic letter. This is what I am inventing. This is not going to work unless you trust the object. √

65. "Cryogenic" freezing is generic freezing with electric current which cures all. It relates to extremely low temperatures. This freezing speed would have to be over a very quick time or the person would not exist. The way it would work is to just freeze the blood in a test tube. Then inject freezing solution into the body: freezing would free-up time so people can find cures to whatever ails the patient. This can be put in their blood. It would use technology of small capsules where they would take the healthy blood cells and analyze how it would be working. This technology is that of which would work. This healthy blood cell would stay frozen. It will use solution cures from one person to give them new life instead of an organ or body part donation. √

66. The new wave radio that has other functions. A list of songs on that way they can download from the internet radio or any other radio station. √

67. Food injected with nutrients. Meat with whatever is in meat the true ingredients. √

68. This invention is super. These are all valuable and real. This means that they will all work.√√

69. Scent-Fresh air freshener air cleaner. Purifies toxins in the air as well as freshens the smell of the environment. √

70. The motor will be filled with water because water is a powerful force. The electrical current will power the engine and the water will be burned and will stay there in the engine and the system will cool the water. The water from the cooling system will be like gasoline for the people. The gas will be water not gasoline which is harmful for animals and the environment. The water will be powered by generators. √

71. This contraption is the scapegoat of modernity. It is the understated power of the few that happens to be good. It is the blame game. It is a board game for individuals to play in their spare time. This is the game of scapegoats: which are people who are individuals who get blamed. This game is for modernity. √

72. This is the automatic tints; this is when it gets bright tinting automatically gets darker. This is in the windows. √

73. This is a universal gift card: any store can have it. It is called the "source card". This card gives out recipes to people from the heart. √

74. This is a bulletproof protection system for cars or anything you need. This protection system protects people from crime. This protection system is legal in the United States. √

75. Night clothing brand. √

76. The invention is a smokeless cigarette. It is a smokeless cigarette. √

77. Automatic organizing file system which automatically organizes files and keeps a number on it. It can then identify who it is by form and number. √

78. The new liquid that cleans out the whole system. It is not a product already conceived but a product of the cleansing of the system. √

79. This is a clean freezer which chemicals in it clean the food fresh forever as well as refrigerator unit and device that clean it. √

81. This is a portable power source battery pack for anything. Very good for money making product ideas is this contraption. It is very useful and good to use on these trips or on anywhere portable which is for any device. It can be used for anything imaginable that you want to use it for including car trips and camping. This is a great idea. √

82. The digital books that have talking receptors. They tell stories to kids of all youth ages. They are digital because it is in the chip.

The books have chips in them that talk to kids and tell them stories that are interactive and fun.√

83. The company for things that make sense to individual minds. This is a company for learning that can become anything it wants. It is an independent learning company that is good for business. It is good for society because it creates thought. It is an independent research service. It researches fully the real facts of modern man. It is to prove history true in the schools and society. √

84. Shirts that is like a pocket protector for men that is waterproof and stained proof. It is an actual pocket that can wrap around pens and keep them securely fastened. It is made of fabric. It is made to secure the type of activity that is under your pants. √

85. This driving navigational system will adjust to the road automatically in automatic mode. It will be easier to drive and will cooperate with this road easily and automatically in an easy manner. This will solve all the problems of a driver. This wireless microphone goes to the headset on a phone. It will speak through the headset to the phone. It will work for anything vice-versa. Then it gives to that interception of the phone to the headset. This message system is a system of messages. This goes directly to your phone and to the headset. I said this because it goes both ways. √

86. This happens to be a pager that is electronic a radio signal sender that sends a message to the cop officers with a phone without having to press a button. This does away with any activity that is legal and the possibility of the mistake of hurting people. By doing this it tells one's location on your site. It is in the cop system at all times. √

These are forever for the attributed realities, of the governing body on the God of the world.

These Endeavors Are Of the Justices And the Accomplishments From Where Inside the System Of Mankind's Dilemma Are That Is This In Choice Or From Whatever Is In These Real World Themes. Where There Comes What Is In An Illusion For Justice And Peace Therein The World. The World's Accomplishments Are Of My Personal Life's Personal Achievements For These Endeavors of Man's Very Accomplishments That Are Not Hidden From God's Promises Forever Inside Of These Life's Accomplishments Of Man.

I have connected well with the Facebook people. I am the best friend of Justin Fanning who knows your daughter. In Highland Park High School I have had many friends and graduated from the "Class of 2000" which the newspaper conned as "The X Generation". The school's graduations were always very top people. Like in the lives and with successes Highland Park High School has graduated the very elite and most spoiled many Highland Park High School students whereof I have earned a reputation.
Am "Best Friends" In Dallas With People Who Know The Same People Who Know Your Daughters – Barbara Bush and One Friend Dated Jenna Hager –
Always Was An Young Life Alumni Where I Became A True Christian Person; In Christ
Went to Kanakuk Camp – Always have had a Christian Relationship With Jesus Christ God and the Holy Spirit- I Want to Write The Last Two Books Of The Holy Bible Called "Accolades I & II"

I Have A Love Of Politics and Your Family – Followed Your Campaign Some – Have Always Been An Avid Supporter – Know

Your Family's Friendships – Have Some Interest In Marrying Your Daughter – Always am a Fellow Conservative – Am A Fellow Christian – Fellow Businessman – Have A Liking For Your Daughter – Have Always Talked Politics; With Many People – Fell In Love With Your Daughter Two Years Ago – Am An HPPC Member -

Family Man Within My Father Tyree Miller Who Knows Many People Like You –
Dallas Texas Resident And From All Of This Comes the Fellow Preston Hollow Person -

The Top Businesses-
I have over, five hundred, and different, qualities and explanations, of the many and consistent business ideas and concepts, of, quality, and on over thirteen different packets, or business sheets, in the quality of the dinosaur's eggs. These are from the parodies and riddles, of these riddles of the Sphinx's directions.

I say this, because these dinosaur's eggs, are of the top rank in the Animal Kingdom, behind the Elephant, Donkey, Serpent, Lion, the Bear, and the Dragon. This is about my journey and in how I want to start schools that are within my secret society social clubs, of the new world order's schooling, to defeat the dragon; in the many ways of schools, in high society, that if, these are started, as schools, then the world will always all, become and follow, thereafter in many schools ways.

Schooling-

My Mission Is That I Want To Be Given The Top Presidential Scholarship For Fine Art And Law Studies At Either the Top School In the World – Or From the School's Graduation That Has All That Have Become Already Established And In Whatever Has Belonged In Great Britain's Finest Students At the University Of, the Real Oxford Inside Of These "Bubble Schools" That I Can Become In To Belong Inside The Riches Of the System From Either Highland Park High School's Top Student's Graduated

Alumni Or From the Riches Of Dallas, Texas, That, I Am Used To, To the University Of Oxford's Successful Students and Graduates, Forever From My Other Life's Missions, That Are To Get Into A School Student's Top Diplomas In the University Level – Highland Park High School Graduate And Alumni - Friends With Many Highland Park People From School - Matriculated To Nation's Top Boarding School – WRA; In Hudson Ohio – Went to Western Reserve Academy Preparatory School Which Was Top Ever – Top America College Testing Score 31 ACT- Chicago Top College Education - College Of Dupage In; Glen Ellyn Illinois - Top Graduate From Nation's Biggest And Best Community College — The Top "Honors Scholar" - Honors Scholar Medal – Phi Theta Kappa Honors Society – The Dean's List – Graduated From Honors Scholar Program – 1st Year Program Person at College of Dupage – Helped Found First Year Of The Elite Honors Scholar Program – High Levels From Teachers – Matriculated To Miami Of Ohio, and Then Left – The Classes Were Too Hard – But, Was the Best Food, Women, and Preppy Lifestyles – It Was Voted All Of This When I Went There In 2005 – I Have Struggled With Severe ADHD My Whole Life And Cannot Heal Because Of Too Much Stress And Strain In My Lives – This Came From Too Much Excitement In The Matriculation To Becoming A Top Student In Life – The Apple That Fell Too Far From the Tree – Almost All Of My Schooling Accepted Me In This Way!

Miami of Ohio Student

Writer of 71 books   - 60 - New World Order Literature Writer

Political-

The New World Order's Top President King Position – Determined Recruiter Have the "A. I. C." - Associated Individual's Club Founder Promoter and Responsible Creator - Skull And Crossbones Secret Society Future Friend – Entrepreneur of the New World Order Attributes --

Skull And Crossbones-

The Standard Elite –The Skull and Crossbones Membership Bible-

Accomplishments:

Gained favoritism at Young Life camp in Saranac, New York, where I became a newborn Christian – and then, a member of God's naturalistic elite. Have, traveled to many countries, including Israel, where I got to see Jesus Christ. Have, maintained and established good relationships with the employees, of Sonny Bryans barbecue, in Dallas. Read over sixty books on philosophy, Christianity, and, mathematics. Became, a Member of Trinity Presbyterian Church, in Hinsdale, Chicago where I met, and befriended Steve Preston, from church studies, and church membership – Mister Steve Preston worked, in your cabinet, in the administration, and, from the "Small Business Administration", and then, became a member of the U. S. Department of Housing and Urban Development, wherein he, became good friends with myself; when I visited him in Washington, D. C., with Mister Tyree Miller, my father. Steve, was hired in the government of yours, after Tyree Miller, befriended him. He was hired at our house in Hinsdale, after a government worker, interviewed him, and, asked him a series of questions, on his life. We worked together on the church, set up crew, where my dad and I, set up chairs and tables, before church everyday. I have made, friends like him everyday of my whole life. In Hinsdale, I volunteered everyday, to the church, and went on many mission trips, and participated in the church to where, all of my hope, and salvation, lies in Jesus Christ. I, have lately been visiting my grandfather, in his "home", at an retirement community, where I have tried to witness, to him, the greater news of his life: in how he can be saved. I have witnessed a view of Heaven, after being a Christian at Young Life camp. Most people, in my life have influenced me because I am an easily influenced person. I, have gone to Kanakuk Kamps, where four times and have always been a popular person, with this camp. I think, a man like Doctor Joe White can easily influence the lives of others, and, can also make me a King. This is also, true of many people in my, life. I just need government workers, and, government correspondents, from your life, that we could hire, and, then put to the job, of the new order of the ages. This could, always be Joe White. I, have always loved and adored, "Coon Creek Club", with my dad, and all, of his friends. I, can make friends easily through my dad, and, I always have made these friends with, his friends. I, have also always mooched off of my dad, at "DCC". Wherein, high school, we would go with our friends, and eat lunch, at the "Men's Grill". I am an avid and lover of golf. I, have worked for Albert Black, the coolest black person, I have ever met, in life. I, have worked for Bill Dunlap and, Ted Case before at "Case Dunlap" and, at "Walraven", Book Cover Company, and have been to many social events and parties at their house. I have influenced and befriended, Jordan Webb, who would like to be a part of the "skull and crossbones" in Dallas, which I plan on to start. This is also true of Justin Fanning. These are my friends from Highland Park High School. These were in my same grade, and graduating class. I, have also met some unusual people, in who I do not want to be in the Dallas "Skull and Crossbones", clubs of mine. I, do obviously want you, and your dad to be a part of this. Steve Preston could be in this also. I, have always planned, to be Valedictorian of the University of Oxford, in Oxford, England. I would, always and also, want to marry your daughter. She has friends, which are friends of mine, in Dallas. How, else am I supposed to run the world, and start the new order of the ages? I have now worked, over almost one year, at "H. I. S. Bridgebuilders", in Dallas, where, there are many Christians from the Ghetto. I, have recently met, many people, who want to be in the "Skull and Crossbones" of Dallas, Texas, and in, where I have met, and some of the people, have met you, in your honor, President George W. Bush Jr. I, plan on writing some of the books of the Bible. This has interested many people. The thing is, I have written so many things, Mister President George W. Bush Jr., that I feel obligated, into, selling this to you. Mostly, the new world order is yours, if you could and would like, to sell this to the world of mine, and yours, from Dallas, to Oxford, to, Santa Fe, New Mexico. This could also bloom, over the world. This "new world order", will happen overnight. This plans for the new order of the ages, is from my very inspiration, and, my very own intelligence, that has been around for ten years. I have seen glory, and greatness, like nothing else, in this. This is always, positive and,

good vibes, which I can always come to work with, and, in that I can always know, about Mr. George W. Bush. To be honest, I have seen it all over the Internet, about, thousands of times. I have told, a story, with my life that can not ever be interpreted, unless by the grace of, Jesus Christ. This is from and in, when you inspired me, with a speech, from the new world order. Then, is from when I turned my life around, and then started living for Jesus Christ. I, was fond of this, after you were elected to President position. But let me make it clear, I want to become the President King. And, this is harder than anything else I have ever seen. My father, Tyree Miller, has paid for most of my things, but I want to become a zillionaire, with all, of your help and support. I, guess you can say I am a popular person. This is from my endings and my beginnings. I have charted out and have mapped out the whole new world order, from the Internet. I have created a whole new world, and a whole new business world. How do I say this; enough to own the world, and enough to hire everyone, and, enough to make "Zillions" of dollars, of world ownership. I have created a whole new world. This, is from the ground of zillions on up. The packet I want to give you, is the whole new plans, for the future history of the world.
I have done most of it all.

I am now running for the future and real <u>President King</u> real position and I have had many trials and tribulations before I have get there inside life. The one position that is the "Top Position in the Government" is about this position. I am thirty male and white and I have connected with personal top connections my whole life that is about me and me only. – The "New World Order" is an, Internet sensations.

Sincerely, Riley Parker Miller.√ XOΩ

To in all: To George W. Bush Jr.

I am a "very well connected" Christian man- I have honors classes in the past former Bible learning and very well taught teachers. This is of the close and personal me.

Some with some friends and residences from and in some of the top personal fun and Christians loving people that is in the world's politicians. Senator Rick Santorum visited our political place and I consider it this because of the top people who have read my skull and crossbones manuals so that I have been connected well with these politics and ideas that have got me this far. Some people at the "Inner City" ministry of the close and beneficial: "H. I. S. Bridgebuilders". West Dallas's Christian Ministry work seems very affective and close with me. I respect and know Jesus Christ as my personal and protective real Lord and Savior's life's goals, that are perfectly perfect, for the fully and known respectful lives, within, these God. X

www.ingramcontent.com/pod-product-compliance
Lightning Source LLC
Chambersburg PA
CBHW071525180526
45171CB00002B/381